RIGHT-SIZED, RIGHT-SKILLED™

The Art and Science of Matching Fractional
Executives with Organizations So That Both Thrive

Henning Schwinum

Right-Sized, Right-Skilled™
The Art and Science of Matching Fractional Executives with
Organizations So That Both Thrive

© 2026 Henning Schwinum

ISBN Paperback: 979-8-9937169-7-8
ISBN Hardback: 979-8-9937169-8-5

Table of Contents

Introduction..5

PART I: Understanding the Fractional Executive Model.................7

Chapter 1: Introduction: A New Era of Leadership..............................9

Chapter 2: What a Fractional Executive Is (and Is Not) 15

Chapter 3: How Fractional Assignments Work...............................22

PART II: The Fractional Executive's Playbook 29

Chapter 4: Becoming a Fractional Executive.................................31

Chapter 5: Building a Business Around Yourself 36

Chapter 6: Winning Fractional Assignments...............................52

Chapter 7: Sustaining Success as a Fractional Leader 66

PART III: The SMB Leader's Guide to Fractional Talent................79

Chapter 8: Why Fractional? 81

Chapter 9: When to Engage a Fractional Executive 97

Chapter 10: How to Integrate a Fractional Leader 111

Chapter 11: The Matchmaking Process.....................................126

Chapter 12: Shared Accountability: How Engagements Succeed......149

PART IV: The Future of Fractional Leadership..........................157

Chapter 13: The Blended Workforce and Beyond.........................159

Introduction

Right-Sized, Right-Skilled™ bridges the fast-growing world of Fractional Executives and the business leaders who depend on them. This book exists to demystify the model—clarifying what Fractional Leadership truly is, how it works, and how both executives and organizations can harness its power for sustainable growth.

For aspiring or active Fractional Executives, Right-Sized, Right-Skilled™ serves as a comprehensive roadmap to building not just a career—but a sustainable business—around one's professional expertise. It guides readers through the critical steps to define a compelling value proposition and position themselves as indispensable partners rather than interchangeable consultants. The book delves deeply into personal branding, exploring how to build visibility and authority through thought leadership, storytelling, and credibility signals that resonate with both investors and Chief Executive Officers (CEO).

It also provides practical guidance on the mechanics of running a fractional business—crafting service models, pricing engagements for value rather than hours, managing client portfolios, and balancing delivery with business development. Readers will learn how to secure recurring assignments, strengthen referral networks, and maintain momentum between engagements. Beyond tactics, it encourages a mindset shift—from employee to entrepreneur—helping Fractional Leaders establish systems, boundaries, and habits that enable long-term success, professional satisfaction, and resilience in a competitive and evolving market.

For founders, owners, and CEOs of small- and medium-sized businesses (SMBs), the book offers practical, experience-based frameworks for understanding when Fractional Leadership makes strategic sense and how to implement it effectively. It begins by helping business leaders recognize the inflection points at which they need senior expertise: when revenue stalls, when the founder-led model begins to strain, or when the organization faces scaling, transformation, or exit preparation. Through examples and diagnostic tools, it illustrates how to evaluate readiness, define desired outcomes, and calculate the true return on investing in Fractional Executive talent.

Once the decision is made, the book outlines a proven process for identifying the right leader, onboarding them for rapid integration, and creating alignment between the Fractional Executive, the CEO, and the internal team. It offers step-by-step guidance for setting goals, managing engagement cadence, measuring results, and maintaining accountability, all while ensuring cultural fit and team cohesion. For leaders seeking growth without overextending resources, this book shows how Fractional Executives can accelerate strategy execution, professionalize key functions, and generate lasting enterprise value, turning temporary engagements into transformative partnerships that endure well beyond their term.

Ultimately, *Right-Sized, Right-Skilled*™ champions a new leadership paradigm, one rooted in flexibility, expertise, and shared success. It challenges outdated notions of full-time permanence and multi-role hustle, revealing how Fractional Executives are reshaping the modern workforce. Whether you're stepping into a fractional role or seeking transformative leadership for your business, this guide provides the clarity, tools, and confidence to make it work so both sides win, and both grow.

PART I

Understanding the Fractional Executive Model

CHAPTER 1

Introduction: A New Era of Leadership

Innovation is often discussed in terms of products, technology, and operations. Organizations invest heavily in improving what they build and how they deliver it. Yet far less attention is paid to how leadership itself evolves as companies grow.

Nowhere is this gap more visible than in the executive leadership of small- and medium-sized businesses. Many organizations continue to rely on outdated models—waiting too long to hire senior leadership or assigning critical responsibilities to individuals without the necessary experience. These approaches create friction, missed opportunities, and stalled growth.

Fractional Leadership emerged to solve this structural problem. It allows companies to access experienced executives at the moment they are needed—without the cost, risk, or rigidity of a full-time hire. What began as a pragmatic solution has evolved into a powerful model for modern growth, reshaping how organizations think about leadership, execution, and scale.

There are those who call me the "granddaddy" of the Fractional Executive world because I've been immersed in this industry since its earliest days. Fractional Leadership, at least as we understand it now, is less than a decade old. While fractional executives have existed for decades in forms such as interim and part-time leadership, the modern, platform-enabled fractional model has accelerated significantly over the last decade. And I've been part of it since 2019, which makes me an early pioneer.

My journey, though, began long before the word "fractional" existed.

For about 25 years, I built a career in sales leadership across chemicals, services, and software. I started at a major German chemical company, selling pigments and later working in supply chain. Then, around 1999, when e-business was exploding much like AI is today, what started as a small side project became my entire job. Within months, I was leading a team and spending nearly all my time figuring out how digital tools could reshape buying, selling, and the supply chain in the chemical industry.

During that period, I met a Kansas City startup building what was essentially "Google for chemists." We became their customer, and six months later, the founder recruited me to build their business in Europe. That marked the beginning of a long chapter in startup life, where sales is everything and growing the business means constantly selling.

Over the next 11 years, I led sales and marketing for the company, first regionally in Europe, then globally as we expanded into Latin America and Asia. Eventually, I ran the U.S. operations as well, even though I was still living in Europe. After the company was acquired, I continued to support the integration of additional acquired businesses. However, over time, my work became repetitive. Managing people, building budgets, and hearing the same familiar excuses no longer taught me anything new.

By 2019, I was ready for a change.

I believed Fractional Sales Leadership could be the next phase of my career: stepping into companies selectively, fixing or building their sales function, then moving on. But when I began exploring that path, two obstacles became obvious.

First, my network wasn't built for fractional opportunities. My LinkedIn[1] connections at the time were mostly other sales leaders, not founders, owners, CEOs, board members, investors, or leaders in the startup ecosystem. Also, fractional work doesn't originate in Fortune 1,000 companies; it starts in early-stage and growth environments, and I wasn't connected to those circles.

Second, I couldn't find a single agency or matchmaker focused on Fractional Sales Executives. Some firms covered the entire C-suite, but sales leadership seemed to always be an afterthought. In many industries, sales leaders aren't even titled as part of the C-suite. Yet fractional roles require specialization and precision, not broad generalist coverage.

My assumption was simple: If I'm struggling to navigate this world, other Fractional Executives must be struggling too.

After a few validation calls, that assumption proved true. Fractional Executives had no structured path to secure assignments, and founders, especially first-time founders and CEOs in family-owned businesses, didn't know how to identify the right Fractional Leader. Most could articulate what they wanted ("grow 50%," "fix sales," "reduce churn") but not what they truly needed. They would default to surface-level requirements: "Has to come from our industry," followed by vague soft traits like "team player" or "superstar" labels so generic they're meaningless.

That gap became the spark.

I'd always wanted to start a business but never felt I had "the big idea." In my first startup experience, I was a builder, not the originator. But in 2019, for the first time, the idea was mine. I realized there was a real

---

[1] https://www.linkedin.com/in/henning-schwinum/

and obvious need for a specialized matchmaker dedicated to Fractional Sales Leadership. That's how **Vendux**[2] was born.

The connection between my past and my new direction was clearer than it seemed. For nearly two decades, I represented a search engine for chemicals. Now I represent a search engine for executives. The industries couldn't be more different, but the mechanics are similar: a two-sided marketplace matching buyers and sellers, in this case, companies and executives. We eventually built our own matching technology because nothing on the market adequately captured the complexity of finding the **right** executive for the **right** situation.

And the right match matters. In Fractional Leadership, success is not simply about hiring someone with experience. It requires alignment between the executive's Superpower, the company's growth stage, its products or services, its challenges, its expectations, and its culture. When the alignment is right, fractional work produces transformative outcomes. When it's not, the relationship quickly sours for everyone involved.

A Superpower is the narrow, repeatable capability a Fractional Executive delivers exceptionally well in specific environments. It is not a job title, seniority level, or collection of experiences, but a proven ability to solve the same class of problems across multiple organizations. Superpowers emerge at the intersection of expertise, pattern recognition, and execution under constraint. Executives who clearly articulate their Superpower— what they do best, for whom, and under which conditions—match faster, deliver results sooner, and avoid misaligned engagements.

Over the last six years, I've watched the fractional space grow at an extraordinary pace. CFOs were the earliest adopters, but companies are

---

[2] https://www.vendux.org/

now hiring Fractional Leaders across sales, marketing, operations, HR, technology, and all other functional areas. Small- and medium-sized businesses especially benefit because their full-time roles often force executives to wear too many different hats. Fractional Leadership allows companies to right-size and specialize their talent: bring in **exactly** the expertise needed, at **exactly** the right moment, for **exactly** as long as it's required.

A company going from $0 to $1M in revenue needs one kind of leader. Scaling from $1 to $5M requires another. Entering a new market, stabilizing churn, rebuilding a broken sales engine, rebranding, or fundraising, each of these scenarios calls for someone who has solved that very problem before. Fractional engagements make this precision possible. They are finite, focused, and tailored to the company's lifecycle.

That's why I see Vendux not as a recruiting firm but as a matchmaker. We don't scour the internet for candidates. We curate a vetted roster of executives and match them with companies based on readiness, experience, and situational fit.

Alongside Vendux, I helped launch **#BeFractional**[3], a training organization for executives entering the fractional world. Many are brilliant subject-matter experts but have never had to build a business around themselves. Fractional work turns executives into solopreneurs, where they are the product. That means learning how to position oneself, build a brand, sell one's expertise, deliver outcomes, and operate with discipline.

As the industry matured, ten companies, including Vendux, joined to form the **Fractional Leadership Alliance**[4], the first global association

---

[3] https://www.befractional.org/
[4] https://www.fractionalleadershipalliance.com/

dedicated to fractional work. As of early 2026, I now serve as its Executive Director. In this early stage, it's a fractional role; it's something I do because the industry needs a gold standard, legitimacy, and most importantly, a collective voice.

Most recently, Vendux acquired **Shiny**[5], a well-known platform connecting businesses with Fractional Executives across the C-suite. Shiny has built a strong reputation for its innovative digital platform, enabling companies to tap into experienced Fractional Leaders.

The real craft of Fractional matchmaking includes translating a CEO's goals into the specific criteria that determine success: product type, price point, decision-maker, deal cycle, industry, stage, team maturity, and ownership model. When all of those align with the experience of a Fractional Executive, that's the perfect match.

There are books already published for executives entering fractional work, as well as for CEOs considering engaging a Fractional. But none of them connect the two sides or detail the **art and science** of making the model succeed. It's not enough to talk about the benefits of Fractional Leadership. Success depends on clear foundations on both sides and on a structured approach to matching executives with organizations so both can thrive. Ultimately, the PerfectMatch™.

In the following chapters, I aim to provide this dual-perspective playbook for executives, for leaders of small- and medium-sized businesses, and everyone else navigating the rapidly evolving world of Fractional Leadership.

---

[5] https://useshiny.com/

CHAPTER 2

What a Fractional Executive Is (and Is Not)

The Fractional Executive model is still new enough that I should provide a clear definition of its exact meaning, as published by the Fractional Leadership Alliance, which centers on two important phrases: "fractional" and "executive."

Fractional means part-time, and in the U.S., Fractional Executives are often structured as 1099 contractors (someone receiving payment based on the 1099-NEC Nonemployee Compensation[6] by the IRS), though legal classification ultimately depends on the specifics of control, scope, and engagement structure; as opposed to W-2 employment (a traditional employee classified by the IRS as a Wage and Tax Statement[7] recipient). Other countries have their own equivalents, but the principle is the same: contract-based part-time work, not full-time employment.

An **Executive** is a leadership role responsible for strategy and leadership of a major function within an organization. In our world at Vendux, fractional roles include a VP of Sales or a Chief Revenue Officer (CRO), as they lead a core function. While any job can be fractionalized, not every part-time role becomes a "Fractional Executive."

When adding talent to a company, the key question for smaller organizations should always be: "How much of this specific skill set do we truly need?"

---

[6] https://www.irs.gov/forms-pubs/about-form-1099-nec
[7] https://www.irs.gov/forms-pubs/about-form-w-2

Smaller companies often have to justify full-time roles by forcing individuals to wear multiple hats. A Chief Financial Officer (CFO) becomes the CFO, Operations Leader (COO), Human Resources Leader (CHRO), and Office Manager. A Sales Leader becomes a "player-coach," carrying a quota while simultaneously leading a team. This multi-hat model is not only inefficient but also risky. For example, HR is a compliance-heavy function; if you don't give it the necessary expertise, you expose yourself to legal risks. Yet in smaller companies, leaders who are not trained in HR often handle all people matters.

Fractionalization solves this problem by right-sizing. You bring in experts for exactly the expertise you need, and nothing more. It is entirely possible for a business to operate with a fully Fractional Leadership team. I work with several founders who still hold full-time jobs while their early-stage companies run with Fractional Executives and contractors. It works because every role is focused, specialized, and sized correctly.

What some people describe as "part-time" in terms of duration is really **interim** work: a designated full-time assignment for a limited period, such as covering maternity or medical leave. Interim work is more common in Europe due to stricter employment laws; companies don't want to hire someone full-time just to cover a leave, because they are then "stuck" with the employee. Fractional work is different. Many fractional assignments are structured as month-to-month, though fixed-term engagements are also present, especially for transformation or transition work.

Fractionals are also often mixed up with advisors and consultants. The Fractional Leadership Alliance brought clarity[8], and here is how

---

[8] https://www.fractionalleadershipalliance.com/thought-leadership

Fractional Executives differ from interim executives, consultants, and advisors:

- **Fractional Executive**: A part-time, senior leader embedded in the organization on an ongoing basis, reporting to the CEO, founder, or board. Fractional Executives hold real decision-making authority, lead teams, and are accountable for outcomes, combining strategic leadership with hands-on execution.
- **Interim Executive**: A full-time executive installed for a fixed period to bridge a transition (e.g., vacancy, leave, acquisition). Like Fractionals, they carry authority and manage teams—but their role is temporary and replacement-oriented, not right-sized.
- **Consultant**: A project-based specialist engaged to deliver defined outputs. Consultants may advise or implement, but they are not embedded leaders, do not own outcomes, and typically exit once the project concludes.
- **Advisor**: A trusted expert providing guidance on an ad hoc basis. Advisors offer insight and perspective but hold no operational responsibility, authority, or team leadership.

From the client's perspective, there are several major advantages to fractional talent:

1. Cost Efficiency

A Fractional Executive is far less expensive than a full-time equivalent. While the hourly rate of a Fractional may sometimes appear high, the true comparison is: Do you actually need and hence have to pay for 40 hours per week? Often, the answer is no.

2. Accelerated Scaling

The alternatives to Fractional hiring are either delaying the hire or forcing one person to take on multiple roles. Both result in slow growth.

A Fractional Leader can build the function earlier and more effectively, enabling a company to scale faster.

3. Speed to Talent

Full-time executive searches take 3–6 months. Fractional Executives can be identified, interviewed, and onboarded within a week.

4. Higher Qualification

Fractional Executives are hired for their experience. They are not being hired for "growth potential." They are hired because they've solved this exact challenge before.

These advantages naturally lead to common questions about who becomes a Fractional Executive. Fractionals usually aren't 27-year-olds; they simply haven't accumulated enough experience. At the same time, someone who has spent 30 years or more at a single corporation is often too entrenched in one system and culture to adapt quickly to the varying nature of Fractional work. The ideal Fractional Executive has breadth in their resume: multiple roles, multiple companies, and exposure to varied organizational challenges, while being able to clearly articulate their Superpowers.

Most Fractionals are in their 40s and 50s, though some highly experienced people already enter the space in their 30s. By the time people reach their 50s, financial volatility is easier to tolerate, with mortgages or college tuition often behind them, and they have the freedom to take career risks. Fractional work requires confidence, adaptability, and the willingness to repeatedly source your own income. It is not a path for the risk-averse or for those looking for financial stability.

The shift toward fractional work is part of a broader change in the modern workplace. The days of spending 30 years at one organization and retiring with a pension are gone for many. The gig economy and the work-from-home movement have transformed how people work, and Fractional Executive Leadership is a natural extension of that evolution. It is an opportunity to apply your skills across multiple companies, avoid stagnation, and solve interesting problems without being trapped within a single corporate culture.

From the employer's perspective, the key to using Fractional Executives effectively is understanding the right size and right skill set. Business owners often assume that more hours equal better outcomes, but that's not always true. If a founder spends 10 hours a week selling and closes five customers in a month, a seasoned sales leader can likely achieve more in those same 10 hours. And on the other hand, spending 40 hours a week selling does not necessarily 4x the outcome. So, you don't need to hire full-time if the work doesn't require it.

Fractional contracts create flexibility. You can start someone at 10 hours a week and adjust up or down based on demonstrated need. Fractional Executives typically manage 2–5 clients[9] at any given time, and they flex those hours as assignments begin, end, and need adjustments. If a client relationship isn't ideal, they can replace that client with another. It's one of the freedoms that make this model so attractive.

When qualifying both executives and clients for a Fractional Sales Leadership engagement, I focus heavily on the sales scenario, the specific environments and conditions the sales function operates in. I ask executives and CEOs about team size, revenue, decision-makers, deal size, sales cycle, and the nature of the product.

---

[9] https://www.vendux.org/2025-state-of-fractional-sales-leadership

This focus on specific environments is intentional. Vague labels like "rock star," "software," or "manufacturing" are often used to signal excellence and fit, but they offer no actionable insight into whether someone will succeed in a particular role. In fractional work, in particular, labels are a liability. Success depends on having solved the client's exact problem in the context of similar deal sizes, decision-makers, sales cycles, and constraints. Fractional Executives are not hired for symbolic status, to fill an empty box on an org chart, or perceived potential; they are hired for proven, situationally relevant experience.

For clients, I assess:

- where they are today in their growth journey,
- what's working and what isn't,
- how complex is the environment they operate in, and
- what is their growth goal over the next 6–12 months.

Most founders start by saying, "We need someone from our industry." But once we unpack the true criteria, industry becomes just one variable. Skills often transfer across verticals much more effectively than people expect.

Fractional work tends to expose executives to far more industries than they'd encounter in a single full-time career. After two or three years, many Fractionals can point to a much broader resume than they ever had before; just another benefit of the model.

Fractional Executives are a strong fit primarily for small- and medium-sized businesses. On the other hand, Fractionals are rarely effective leading core, ongoing functions in Fortune 1,000 organizations, though they are sometimes used for scoped initiatives, transitions, or special projects. Large organizations require extensive internal onboarding for an executive just to function, and Fractionals are brought in to deliver results immediately, not study org charts for six months.

Consequently, the Window of Opportunity for a Fractional Executive is driven by company size, but it varies by function. Many $1M businesses may not yet require a fractional CFO, though complexity, capital structure, or growth plans can justify one earlier. But at $5–10M, a fractional CFO becomes critical. For sales leadership, I place Fractionals in companies from pre-revenue to those having 7 or 8 sales reps. By that point, most companies need a full-time leader, and the fractional window closes.

The Window of Opportunity describes the specific period in a company's lifecycle when Fractional Leadership delivers maximum impact. This window is not defined by time alone, but by the intersection of business stage, complexity, urgency, and readiness. It opens when a company's needs outgrow founder-led execution or functional improvisation yet does not justify full-time executive headcount. It closes when scale, team size, or operational stability requires permanent leadership.

Fractional Executives thrive where expertise matters more than headcount and where focus matters more than hierarchy. And on both sides, the executive and the employer, the goal is the same: **the right size, the right skill, and the PerfectMatch**™

CHAPTER 3

How Fractional Assignments Work

In the early years of Vendux, I had to actively reach out to Fractional Executives, mainly through LinkedIn, explaining what I was building and asking whether they were open to a conversation. But in recent years, that's changed. Today, executives find us organically through search, artificial intelligence (AI), and word of mouth.

There has been a notable increase in the number of professionals entering fractional work. And many find themselves underutilized in their current assignments and eager to fill their calendars.

Right now, early in 2026, the market is imbalanced: supply has grown much faster than demand, though I believe this is a temporary situation. Some executives are finding it difficult to secure enough assignments and are returning to full-time roles. Currently, about 15–20 out of every 100 who join our roster eventually shift back. Over time, supply and demand will naturally realign as unsuccessful Fractionals exit and overall market awareness and assignment opportunities grow.

By my estimation, only about 15% of small- and medium-sized businesses in the U.S. have used a Fractional Executive. That leaves an enormous 85%, or around 2.6 million companies, that could benefit from Fractional Leadership but simply haven't been exposed to it. The biggest barrier is education.

That's why ten companies, including Vendux, formed the Fractional Leadership Alliance (FLA) in 2024. The purpose is to unify and amplify messaging, speak on behalf of the industry, and accelerate market adoption. The FLA includes matchmakers, training organizations, directories, and community platforms across multiple functions, including sales, marketing, finance, operations, and beyond.

When a founder, owner, or CEO comes to Vendux with an opportunity, we begin by scoping the assignment in detail. We explore:

- Where sales stand today
- The growth targets for the next 6–12 months
- Sales history and performance
- Current team structure and skill sets
- Customer base and revenue
- Ideal Client Profile (ICP) and personas
- Existing systems and processes
- The specific past experiences and capabilities required for the success of the Fractional

All of this results in a scope document that serves as the foundation for matching.

We then feed the scope into our proprietary software system, which evaluates and scores more than 80 criteria and produces a ranked list of executives. From the top candidates, we reach out to three to five and gauge interest and availability. Those who are interested and aligned are introduced to the client.

Matching goes far deeper than industry experience. Key considerations include:

- Owner/operator structure vs. VC/private equity governance
- Product type: SaaS vs. manufactured goods vs. services
- Decision maker persona familiarity: who is being sold to
- Deal type: transactional vs. long-cycle enterprise
- Global vs. local target markets

- Size and complexity of the organization

And in case you are missing it on the list: The myth of the Rolodex is outdated. What matters is the executive's ability to identify and reach the right decision-makers, not a static list of names whose roles have expired.

In around 90% of fractional assignments, location is not a factor. Fractional roles are overwhelmingly remote, especially in Software-as-a-Service (SaaS), Tech, and other like industries. Travel is relevant only for specific use cases, such as quarterly reviews, initial training, or client meetings. Only about 10% of all fractional roles require a local executive, typically because the job depends on local presence and networking.

Assignments proceed to contract once the executive is selected. The contract typically outlines:

- Independent contractor status
- A Statement of Works (SOW) with milestones
- Time expectations (e.g., weekly or monthly hours or specific days)
- Reporting structure
- Compensation (typically a monthly retainer paid in advance)
- Duration (fixed-term or month-to-month)

Retainers are the predominant compensation model because they allow predictable time allocation and straightforward billing.

As they start the assignment, the Fractional Executive should be introduced by the CEO exactly as a full-time equivalent would be: "This is our new Chief Marketing Officer (CMO)." They are not consultants who deliver a PowerPoint deck and then disappear. They step into leadership, inherit a team, own outcomes, and act within the hierarchy.

To support this, the FLA has published **best practices for onboarding Fractionals**[10], focused on employer responsibility, clear communication, expectation setting, and a transparent introduction to the organization.

Fractional Executives on the other hand must enter with clarity and self-awareness. They need to:

- Know their true Superpowers: the problems they solve best and for whom.
- Avoid accepting roles that aren't a fit.
- Be transparent about their strengths, weaknesses, and failure points.
- Clearly explain what conditions must exist for them to succeed.
- Communicate proactively, often through weekly updates or short video summaries.

Executives who try to be "everything to everyone" are rarely successful since fractional work requires precision.

Clients must match that transparency. They must openly communicate about:

- Team strengths and weaknesses
- Broken systems, outdated processes, or missing tools
- Realistic goals, not wishful or investor-driven targets
- Cultural norms and dynamics
- Organizational structure, including ownership and board influence

Unreasonable expectations doom assignments before they start.

---

[10] https://www.fractionalleadershipalliance.com/thought-leadership

While on assignment, Executives should not assume that clients know what they're working on. Weekly communication, as a call, meeting, short video, or email, prevents drift and ensures alignment. It gives clients a chance to redirect priorities before weeks of effort are wasted.

Assignments end for many reasons:

- The business has scaled and now requires a full-time hire
- The executive is converted to full-time (when both parties want it).
- The project is complete (e.g., a sales playbook or strategic buildout).
- The match wasn't perfect and either party chooses to exit.

There should be a full review at the end of every engagement, comparing results to the original scope document, to evaluate success and continuously refine the matching process.

Case Examples

- A client needed a **sales playbook** to support hiring 100 new reps. A Fractional Sales Leader created the structure, documentation, and rollout in three months.

  Takeaway: This case demonstrates how a Fractional Executive can create scalable structure quickly without requiring long-term headcount.

- A client required structure after **losing a founding sales leader.** A fractional VP of Sales built the foundation over 12 months and helped hire his full-time replacement.

Takeaway: Fractional Leadership provides continuity and stability during leadership gaps while preparing the organization for a permanent successor.

- A client, operating in a highly specialized niche, has used a Fractional Executive for four years, proof that **some roles will never require full-time headcount**.

  Takeaway: Some leadership roles are structurally better suited to fractional capacity, proving that "temporary" does not mean short-lived.

- A client scaling rapidly had **outgrown founder-led operations**. A fractional COO implemented process discipline, Key Performance Indicators (KPIs), and cross-functional cadence within 90 days.

  Takeaway: Fractional Leaders excel at professionalizing operations at inflection points where founders can no longer scale the business alone.

- A client with a product-led business needed to **modernize its platform** before scaling. A fractional Chief Technology Officer (CTO) led architecture redesign and vendor selection.

  Takeaway: Fractional expertise allows companies to make critical architectural decisions without the risk or cost of a premature full-time hire.

- A client with an inconsistent pipeline required **sharper positioning and demand generation**. A fractional CMO rebuilt messaging and lead programs in one quarter.

Takeaway: Focused, senior-level marketing leadership can unlock growth faster than incremental campaign execution.

- A client experiencing rapid growth **lacked hiring structure, compliance, and performance management**. A fractional CHRO built recruiting, onboarding, and management systems within three months.

  Takeaway: Fractional HR leadership mitigates compliance and talent risk precisely when informal people practices begin to break down.

- A client preparing for the next growth phase **lacked forecasting and cash-flow visibility**. A fractional CFO implemented financial models and dashboards in 60 days.

  Takeaway: Fractional finance leadership creates decision clarity and confidence long before a company is ready for a full-time CFO.

PART II

The Fractional Executive's Playbook

CHAPTER 4

Becoming a Fractional Executive

When executives first learn about Fractional Leadership, the question that always follows is simple: How do I actually become a Fractional Executive?

One of the first things to understand is that "Fractional Executive" is not a protected term. Anyone can declare themselves a Fractional Executive, but that doesn't make it true. Not every contractor, part-timer, gig worker, advisor, consultant, or coach qualifies. A Fractional Executive must meet the definition shared in Chapter 2: a part-time executive leading a major business function with strategic and operational accountability. Only those who truly fit that description should use the title.

From a business standpoint, a Fractional Executive should operate under a Limited Liability Company (LLC) for liability protection and professionalism. They also need proper professional liability insurance, since their work involves advising companies and influencing decisions that carry real financial consequences.

But formalities aside, the most important requirement is commitment. True fractional work cannot be a side project while holding a full-time job. You must publicly identify as a Fractional Executive, articulate your Superpower, describe the problems you solve, and present yourself professionally on platforms like LinkedIn. In short, you must put yourself out there, not just quietly be available.

How someone transitions into fractional work varies. Some simply quit their job and start their legal entity, though that's the riskiest path. A more thoughtful approach is to anticipate a transition, such as during an acquisition, and use the runway to prepare. If a sale of the company you are working for is coming in six months, you can begin positioning now: refine your profile, build your network, develop your messaging, and let people know you will be available soon.

There's also a third path many people don't consider: turning your current employer into your first client. You can propose a structured transition plan, help identify and onboard your successor, stay on for a defined period, and then transition to a part-time contractor role focused on a specific set of responsibilities. This softens the exit for both sides and provides immediate income stability. It's a professional, mutually beneficial way to begin a fractional career.

One of the biggest challenges that Fractional Executives who are starting out face, especially those coming from corporate roles, is not having the right network. A strong, truly valuable network is essential. Early in my career, when I worked in the same vertical for more than 25 years, I never thought much about networking. For years I declined most LinkedIn requests and ended up with only a few hundred connections, very few of whom were helpful when I launched my fractional journey. They were peers, colleagues, and clients, but not founders, owners, CEOs, investors, or board members.

When I pivoted, I realized how unprepared I was. So, for anyone considering fractional work, especially those with time to plan, I strongly recommend building your network deliberately: founders, CEOs, business owners, investors, advisors, and other Fractional Executives. Today, I have thousands of connections, but that growth took years and intentional effort.

LinkedIn is critical. In my world, if you don't have a LinkedIn profile, it raises red flags. Before any type of call, I check someone's profile. If I can't find it, the first thing I ask is how to locate them. A LinkedIn profile is essentially a living resume that follows someone throughout their career and is far more useful than the shoe boxes of paper business cards many of us used to keep.

In contrast, platforms such as Indeed[11] and Fiverr[12] are not meaningful sources of Fractional Executive opportunities. They're oriented toward full-time or gig work rather than executive-level Fractional Leadership. Fractional opportunities are found through networking, referrals, and specialized platforms such as Shiny or Vendux. Even then, most matches still come through relationships, referrals, and networking, not marketplace postings.

Getting started follows a set of clear best practices: forming a legal entity, securing insurance, defining your Superpower, identifying your ideal customer profile, optimizing your LinkedIn presence, and committing publicly to the fractional path. A true Fractional Executive cannot simply be someone between two full-time roles. Clients want long-term commitment, not someone using fractional work as a stopgap until they find their next W-2 job.

When executives express interest in joining our Vendux roster, we begin with a 30-minute discovery call. That call is largely about helping them understand what we do, how we work, and whether our model aligns with their goals. If we decide to move forward, we schedule an onboarding session, usually 60 to 90 minutes, focused entirely on their experience, strengths, sales scenarios they managed, leadership history, compensation preferences, and target roles. These details help us determine where they fit on our roster and which opportunities are best suited to them.

---

[11] https://www.indeed.com/
[12] https://www.fiverr.com/

Most people then want to know: How long will it take to land my first fractional assignment?

There is no definitive answer. Some executives get matched immediately, sometimes during the onboarding call. Others may wait months. I've seen cases where someone took a full year to close their first assignment, despite doing all the right things. It is important to note that there is an emotional toll from this rollercoaster: the highs of being fully booked and the lows of suddenly having only 50% utilization. The volatility of Fractional Executive assignments is real.

Matching executives with companies is more about timing than it is in traditional recruiting. A company's Window of Opportunity for Fractional Leadership opens and closes almost unpredictably. Unlike software sales, where you can relentlessly target anyone who fits the ideal client profile, we can't simply cold call a founder and say, "You need a fractional sales leader." So, we create visibility and relationships, and then we receive inbound inquiries, often from someone who's been following us on LinkedIn or reading the newsletter for years and suddenly realizes the time is right.

Each fractional function has its own window. A fractional CFO usually comes in at around $5M–$10M in annual revenue and the role can remain fractional until $30M–$40M. A Fractional Sales Leader can be brought in pre-revenue but becomes less viable once a team grows to seven or eight full-time reps. CMOs and COOs have their own windows. CTOs often have the widest window, sometimes spanning from pre-product to well into scaling.

There are outliers at $100M or more of annual revenue that bring in a Fractional Executive, but those roles typically focus on expansions, new product lines, or restructuring rather than leading a core business function. But those use cases are great examples of the versatility of the Fractional Executive solution.

Across the full spectrum, the matching process remains the same: right size, right skill, right time. Our software evaluates multi-criteria inputs and often surprises me by identifying executives I wouldn't have immediately considered. That's the power of removing human bias. I no longer prejudge or fall prey to recency bias. I trust the system to bring the perfect match to the surface.

And of course, once names are presented, the executive and client meet for one or more interviews. When several finalists check every box, the decision can come down to intangible factors or changing variables, such as the willingness to work for equity rather than cash. Compensation structure matters greatly and must be evaluated carefully; equity can be lucrative years down the line, but it carries its own risks.

Ultimately, the Fractional Executive path offers significant opportunities, but it requires clarity about one's Superpowers, commitment, and a willingness to embrace uncertainty. The work is challenging, meaningful, and dynamic, but it is not for everyone. Understanding the realities, both the rewards and the volatility, is essential for anyone considering this career path.

CHAPTER 5

Building a Business Around Yourself

When executives transition into Fractional Leadership, many underestimate just how different this path is from traditional employment. Establishing yourself as a Fractional Executive means building a business, not just offering a service. And like any business, it requires intentional decisions about positioning, pricing, branding, operations, risk, and focus. Most executives, no matter how successful their career has been, have never done this before. So, the learning curve is real.

This chapter walks through how to build that business, including how to position yourself, price your work, sell with confidence, choose the right engagements, and put the operational foundation in place.

No executive is born a Fractional. They become one, usually because they have deep subject-matter expertise, not because they already know how to run a business built around themselves. The identity shift from expert to entrepreneur is foundational.

One of the first changes executives must embrace is how they present themselves. In fractional work, a classic resume is far less useful and the focus should be on a role-relevant profile. Fractional engagements are highly specific, so every introduction we prepare at Vendux is tailored to a particular role.

Becoming a Fractional Executive means you are no longer selling a career history. For many executives, this moment represents a deeper shift than a new career model. It is the point at which they stop identifying primarily as an employee with a title and begin operating as a business of one. As the adage says, "hanging out your shingle," in this sense, is not a marketing act but rather a declaration of independence and accountability. From that point forward, clarity, professionalism, and self-direction are no longer optional; they define how the market experiences you.

Authenticity is foundational to this process. Executives who embrace who they truly are rather than trying to imitate a corporate archetype communicate more clearly, resonate more deeply with CEOs, and build trust faster. Authenticity strengthens positioning by aligning your message with your actual strengths, motivations, and working style. You are selling a productized version of yourself. That requires clarity about what you do, for whom, and what outcomes you deliver. Your positioning is part of your "business architecture," not just your messaging.

In fractional engagements, authenticity accelerates trust. CEOs are not hiring development potential; they are hiring immediate impact. Executives who present themselves honestly reduce friction, shorten decision cycles, and enter engagements with clearer expectations on both sides.

Instead of listing 25 years of experience, identify the three or four roles most relevant to the opportunity at hand. Executives with long corporate histories also need to recognize that earlier stages of their careers quickly become irrelevant. If someone worked at IBM 20 years ago, that experience rarely carries useful weight in today's fractional market.

Experienced Fractional Executives often maintain multiple one-page bios, each tailored to a vertical or specialty they serve. For example, a SaaS founder doesn't care that someone spent 15 years in insurance;

they only care about the candidate's SaaS experience. Positioning is about relevance, not volume.

Becoming the product isn't intuitive for most executives. Marketing, positioning, and even selling yourself can feel awkward at first. But the fractional model demands it: you must articulate your value clearly, confidently, and consistently, just as any business markets its product.

Once the positioning is clear, the next challenge becomes translating that clarity into economic reality. Before speaking to even a single potential client, a Fractional Executive must decide:

- What compensation structures will they accept
- Which will they absolutely not
- What their rates and boundaries are

You cannot "figure it out as you go" because that often leads to bad deals and seller's remorse.

Pricing is not a number; it is a process. You work through it intentionally by defining your financial goals, value, availability, capacity, and target market. Executives who treat pricing as "the number I say on the call" almost always underprice themselves and, as a result, attract the wrong clients.

Fractional compensation, documented in a pricing matrix, can include one or more elements:

- Monthly retainer
- Hourly rate
- Variable components (commission, bonuses)
- Equity (rare and should be considered cautiously)
- Project fees

Industry benchmarks give helpful context. Over the course of the past couple of years, more and more of those benchmarks have been developed, and they can provide the much-needed guidance for a Fractional Executive just starting out. Begin by understanding the context of the benchmark, e.g., the region, industry, year, or role the data was collected from, and then put it to use for yourself. Here are some data points from a 2025 study of Fractional Sales Leadership roles in North America[13]:

- Average hourly rate: **$225/hour**
- Average monthly compensation for a fractional engagement: **$11,732**
- Retainers are used in **88%** of engagements
- Average length of a fractional engagement: **9.7 months**
- Average time commitment for a fractional engagement: **14.6 hours/week**

Benchmarks are not meant to become the pricing matrix, but they can help to anchor one's personal expectations in market reality.

A retainer is paid in advance, usually monthly, and must include clear parameters such as hours per week, days of availability, predefined time blocks, and, of course, a Statement of Work that outlines the assignment goals. In fractional work, ambiguity creates misalignment, so contracts must clearly define the scope, structure, expectations, and goals from the outset.

Executives often seek guidance on pricing because, for many, it is their first time setting prices for themselves and their services.

---

[13] https://www.vendux.org/2025-state-of-fractional-sales-leadership

A starting point for a Fractional Executive is translating a target annual salary, a number most executives are very familiar with, into an hourly rate:

- Take total annual on-target earnings (Base Salary + Target Variable Pay)
- Divide by ~2,100 working hours
- Apply a factor of 1.5x to 2x

The above factor accounts for benefits, business expenses, taxes, and the fact that a Fractional Executive will not be consistently working 40+ hours per week for clients. There is the need to spend time on business development, as well as account for potential downtime.

The full-time on-target earnings alone cannot be used as a proxy for fractional pricing. A $200K a year full-time leader costs a business closer to $300K–$350K when taxes, benefits, paid time off, onboarding, equipment, and unproductive hours are calculated. Fractional Executives must charge for all of this to account for business expenses, risk, non-billable hours, pipeline maintenance, etc., on their end; and to create a true apples-to-apples comparison to the equivalent full-time scenario for the company.

But executives must also consider whether the type of role they're seeking actually aligns with their past compensation. The compensation for running a global organization with 50 people and $200M in annual revenue full-time does not translate directly into a fractional assignment at a $5M company. Smaller companies are less complex and, consequently, have different pay bands.

The pricing for a Fractional Executive in a particular role should reflect:

- Industry

- Geography
- Stage of the company
- The role's scope, responsibility, and complexity
- The value the Executive is asked to generate for the client

Pricing must reflect a combination of market realities and personal business strategy. No Fractional Executive prices themselves in a vacuum. Every rate is shaped by external conditions, as well as internal considerations, and the strongest pricing decisions acknowledge both.

Externally, the market sets certain boundaries. Some industries simply command higher rates than others. For example, SaaS and financial services often pay three to four times more than construction, manufacturing, or nonprofit work, not because the talent is inherently better, but because the economic models are different.

Geography plays a similar role. A founder in the Bay Area or New York expects pricing that reflects a higher cost of living and a more competitive talent market. In contrast, a founder in the Midwest or Southeast may operate within a lower budget.

Company stage also matters: an early-stage startup with no revenue cannot price leadership the same way a growth-stage organization can. And then there's the scope and value the Executive generates. Leading a team of one looks very different from leading a global team of twenty.

But Fractional Executives bring their own internal considerations to the table as well. A fractional business must be structured to sustain the lifestyle, financial goals, and approach to work of the person running it. That means getting clear on your required minimum monthly income, your confidence in your value, your tolerance for risk, the real cost of running your business (taxes, benefits, downtime, tools), and your preferred ideal client profile. A Fractional Executive who thrives in high-growth environments will price differently than someone who prefers steady-state organizations. Similarly, someone who wants only two deep client engagements at any given time will price differently from someone who prefers four to six lighter-touch roles.

These are some of the **internal factors**:

- Cost of living/lifestyle requirements
- Business expenses
- The sense of self-worth
- Risk tolerance
- Lifestyle considerations
- The selected and desired ICP

Fractional pricing sits precisely at the intersection of both sets of factors, internal and external. If your price is solely based on external market benchmarks, you risk underpricing your value or building a business model you cannot sustain. If you price only based on your own financial goals or confidence, you risk drifting out of alignment with what the market is actually able and willing to pay. The strongest pricing strategies balance both, anchored in the market, but calibrated to support the business you are building for yourself.

Executives should prepare a written pricing sheet, not to share as a price list with a client, but to keep front and center, visible at all times, and refer to it when speaking with clients. Otherwise, saying "approximately" or "flexible" signals insecurity and invites negotiation. Documented prices project confidence and clarity.

- Ranges ("It's usually between $6–10K") almost always lead clients to anchor on the lower number.
- Soft language invites haggling.
- Clear numbers signal seniority, expertise, and boundaries.

If there is a large gap between the client's budget and the Fractional Executive's rate, the solution is not to reduce the executive's fee (but rather to revisit the scope). Discounts devalue the offer and permanently anchor the client to a lower number. What they hear is not "discounted price" or "to get us started," but rather simply "price." You will not be able to increase that price later.

Fractional Executives must learn to sell without discomfort, using a multichannel approach, referrals, visibility, and value-driven interactions to build a steady pipeline. Selling yourself is not "sleazy," and it does not have to be "salesy"; it is the natural extension of becoming the product. That confidence comes not from visibility alone, but from preparation. Declaring yourself available before your positioning, scope, and value proposition are clearly defined creates friction rather than opportunity.

Selling, like pricing, is not an event; it's a discipline.

Once conversations begin, the difference between momentum and misalignment comes down to how well expectations are qualified and communicated.

One of the strongest tools in these conversations is storytelling. Human beings remember stories far more readily than credentials. Fractional Executives who can share concise, relevant stories, "a time I solved this exact problem," or "a client who faced the same challenge," create emotional connection, credibility, and clarity. Stories translate expertise into outcomes that founders can visualize, making the value proposition tangible.

For founders, owners, and CEOs, stories reduce perceived risk. Hearing how a similar problem was solved in a comparable environment helps them visualize outcomes and feel safer making the decision. Stories don't replace credentials; they contextualize them.

Fractional Executives must build fluency in sales and marketing because sustaining a fractional business requires an active funnel, prospecting discipline, and the ability to pitch and close engagements. Most executives have never needed to self-generate demand before, but in fractional work, these skills are essential to success.

Equally important is developing resilience. Fractional work brings natural cycles of momentum followed by periods of quiet. Prospects go dark, deals stall, and opportunities fall through with no clear explanation. Unlike corporate environments where structure and regular paychecks buffer uncertainty, Fractional Executives must learn to navigate these fluctuations with steadiness and perspective. Treating setbacks as data rather than personal failure preserves motivation, protects confidence, and keeps the business moving forward.

And just as important as generating the right opportunities is knowing which ones not to pursue.

Culture matters in fractional work, but not in the same way it does in full-time hiring. For short-term, outcome-driven assignments, capability and relevant experience far outweigh personality alignment or team chemistry. Fractional roles exist to solve specific problems, not to establish long-term cultural integration.

That said, culture still functions as a hard "no-go." If something feels off, when the executive or the client senses issues such as defensiveness, lack of trust, unrealistic expectations, or dismissiveness toward expertise, that instinct should not be ignored. Discomfort at the outset often signals deeper misalignment that will surface later as disagreement, scope conflict, or breakdown in communication.

Once an opportunity clears that no-go threshold, however, the remaining evaluation should focus squarely on functional relevance and execution.

Team-wide meet-and-greets, personality tests, and prolonged cultural assessments rarely add value in fractional engagements and often delay decisions unnecessarily.

The discipline is knowing the difference: culture should protect you from bad engagements, not distract you from great ones.

Fractional Executives must be selective, and more importantly, they must know when to walk away. Desperation often leads to poor matches, and poor matches drain time, energy, and credibility. Walking away early prevents wasted weeks of writing proposals, drafting scopes, and building plans for an opportunity that was never viable from the start. "Win fast, lose faster" is the healthiest and most profitable approach.

At the same time, Fractional Executives must cultivate adaptability, the skill to adjust to different business models, leadership styles, and organizational cultures. Versatility helps an executive diagnose challenges and deliver value across varied environments, and the more exposure they gain through training and case studies, the stronger this capability becomes. Still, adaptability has limits, and knowing where those limits are is essential to recognizing when an opportunity simply isn't a fit.

A strong qualification of a fractional engagement also depends on active listening and empathy. Founders, owners, and CEOs often describe symptoms rather than root causes of their challenges, and they often anchor on solutions they think they want rather than those the business truly requires. Fractional Executives who listen deeply, ask clarifying questions, and attune themselves to the pressures the founder is facing gain clearer insight into whether an engagement is viable.

Active listening does more than improve scoping; it prevents misalignment, unrealistic expectations, and future frustration. It helps the executive differentiate between a role that is simply challenging and one that is fundamentally unworkable. Empathy creates understanding; discernment creates protection.

However, there are also situations where a Fractional Executive should decline an engagement, such as:

- The vertical or industry is not of interest
- The founder creates discomfort or raises early red flags
- Compensation falls below the executive's minimum threshold
- The risk of the assignment is disproportionately placed on the executive
- Timelines or expectations are unrealistic

And there is another criterion that is equally important: **the business itself must be capable of supporting success.** A Fractional Executive can only be effective if the company's economics, structure, and timeline make the mandate achievable.

Many early-stage founders believe a Fractional Leader can produce revenue or savings immediately and on their own. In reality, results depend on sales cycles, product readiness, market position, team maturity, and the company's financial runway. When Vendux screens clients, we evaluate not only the role but also whether the business model can sustain and justify the engagement.

A few targeted questions reveal the truth very quickly:

- *How long does your sales cycle truly take—from first touch to signed deal?*
- *How quickly have you historically closed new clients?*
- *What evidence supports your revenue or growth expectations?*
- *What is the buying cycle of your customers?*
- *What is the nature of your vendor contracts?*

- *How much cash runway or operating capital supports the investment in the Fractional Executive?*
- *Which constraints, budget, staffing, product readiness, and tooling cannot be changed?*

These questions help determine whether success is structurally possible or whether the founder is hoping for outcomes that defy economic reality.

A fractional engagement cannot succeed if success requires a miracle. For example, if timelines are too short, cash is too tight, the product is not ready, or the scope demands results the business cannot support, the right decision for both sides is to walk away early. When the business model itself is the obstacle, no level of expertise can overcome it.

Walking away in these situations is not a failure; it is a sign of professionalism, discernment, and long-term business health. Walking away also protects reputation. Fractional Executives are judged not only by results, but by the engagements they choose. Poor matches often lead to strained relationships and weak referrals, while disciplined selection compounds trust and credibility over time.

Building a Fractional Business: The Foundation

As discussed earlier, expertise alone isn't enough. Most Fractional Executives enter fractional work as exceptional subject-matter experts but inexperienced business owners. Success in fractional work also demands continuous learning. The fractional landscape evolves quickly with new tools, emerging markets, shifting expectations, and changing client needs. Executives who commit to ongoing development, peer learning, and skill refinement stay relevant and competitive. A growth mindset ensures that experience compounds rather than stagnates.

The skills that made them successful in corporate roles, such as strategy, leadership, and domain excellence, do not automatically translate into running a lean, sustainable solo business. Many executives discover quickly that they must define and execute a Go-To-Market (GTM) strategy, marketing, sales, operational design, and personal brand building to succeed in the fractional landscape.

This is why structured learning becomes so valuable. No one succeeds in fractional work through instinct alone. A blueprint, a systematic framework for building and operating a business of one, shortens the learning curve and replaces trial-and-error with proven methods. Formal fractional training programs help executives understand the model, avoid common missteps, and develop the discipline required to operate across multiple clients.[14]

Before they can win assignments, executives need several foundational components in place, as outlined earlier in the chapter:

- LLC formation
- Liability Insurance ("Errors and Omissions")
- Defined Ideal Client Profile (ICP)
- Clear articulation of their Superpower
- Succinct positioning statement
- Documented pricing matrix
- Defined go-to-market approach

Fractional Executives also need foundational legal and financial literacy. Understanding contract structures, terms of service, intellectual property rights, and risk allocation protects both the executive and the business. Fractional work introduces legal nuances that many executives have not

---

[14] https://www.befractional.org/

encountered in corporate roles, making legal awareness an essential part of building a sustainable practice.

I refer to this entire process as creating your "suit," the identity and structure you bring into every conversation. Your Superpower should fit into your LinkedIn headline, with supporting detail underneath. The legal entity that you use to offer your fractional services is the most recent in your list of experiences. Your suit also includes your written pricing matrix, outlining your retainer options, hourly rate, project fees, success fees, and equity parameters. And you have a one-page bio with your relevant experiences ready to share with a potential client.

Without this overall clarity, executives struggle to evaluate opportunities, communicate value, negotiate terms, or close the right clients.

Back-Office, Operations & Taxes

Many first-time Fractionals underestimate the back-office tasks. But they're manageable with intention:

- Accounting
- Invoicing
- Receipt tracking
- Taxes, especially quarterly payments

Because retainers can be substantial, a portion should be set aside immediately in a separate account for tax obligations. Paying on a regular schedule prevents penalties and keeps cash flow predictable. Failing to set aside taxes is one of the most common early mistakes.

Most Fractionals handle their own operations at first. As the business grows, they may outsource selectively, though the volume for a solopreneur should never be overwhelming. Building these operational muscles early prevents feast-and-famine cycles and creates the foundation for sustainable growth as the fractional business expands beyond one or two clients.

Brand Building: What It *Really* Means

Branding is often misunderstood. For Fractional Executives, branding is not about logos, colors, or websites. Those things rarely attract clients.

Branding is:

- Stating clearly what you do,
- for whom you do it,
- and what outcome you deliver.

For example:

"I help early-stage fintech founders grow from zero to their first million."

That is far more powerful—and far more relevant—than saying:

"I'm a fractional CRO, ex-Google, ex-Dell, ex-LinkedIn."

Big-company logos rarely impress SMB founders or owners; in many cases, they signal a mismatch. Small- and medium-sized companies operate differently. A leader from a Fortune 100 company is perceived as lacking the hands-on, scrappy, resource-constrained experience needed in early-stage environments.

Branding becomes effective when it is descriptive, outcome-focused, and relatable to the ICP. It also requires understanding of where your buyers are, how they make decisions, and what channels they trust. That means defining buyer personas, identifying visibility platforms, and deliberately showing up. Being in-person or virtual in those communities, content channels, or marketplaces where your ideal clients already spend time. Branding is not just what you say about yourself; it's where and how often the right people encounter you.

Content helps, but the core of fractional brand building is network-driven credibility.

A strong support network strengthens a Fractional Executive's trajectory. Peer communities and training cohorts provide ongoing opportunities to learn from others, compare approaches, and collectively navigate challenges. Mentorship from seasoned Fractionals builds confidence and accelerates capability in ways that solitary effort cannot.

Building a business around yourself is not about becoming louder—it's about becoming clearer, more intentional, and more selective.

CHAPTER 6

Winning Fractional Assignments

This chapter explains how Fractional Executives win assignments in a competitive market. It walks through how executives differentiate themselves, articulate value, navigate interviews, scope engagements, build trust quickly, and manage the realities of selling and delivering fractional work. Rather than focusing on theory or tactics in isolation, this chapter outlines the full lifecycle from first conversation to signed contract and early execution, highlighting where opportunities are won, where they are lost, and how experienced Fractionals approach each step with discipline and clarity.

When executives ask how to secure fractional assignments, the first truth they must accept is simple: there are never too many opportunities. Fractional work is competitive, and the landscape has shifted dramatically over the last several years. In 2022, when we spoke to a client, Vendux was often the only organization they were talking to. Today, that is no longer the case. Clients interview multiple executives and evaluate several matchmakers. As a result, winning roles now requires, more so than a few years ago, differentiation, clarity, and a strong, trust-driven sales process.

Before disciplined interviewing can deliver assignments, executives must clearly articulate their value. Clients are not evaluating experience in the abstract; they want to know whether the executive has solved their specific problem before. An outcome-focused value proposition keeps the conversation grounded and prevents interviews from turning into resume reviews.

Clients will come into interviews with a list of concrete, measurable requirements, and executives should expect to be evaluated against them.

This list will focus on:

- Relevant experience
- Industry alignment
- Functional accomplishments
- Relevant environments
- Specific outcomes previously delivered
- Other skills

It should not include soft filters like likability or long-term cultural fit. Fractional roles are not about the Executive's growth potential or 10-year relationships; they exist to solve a specific problem right now. Both sides must treat interviews with the rigor of full-time hiring, but with a short-term, outcome-driven focus.

Executives must understand this, too. They need to highlight direct experience, not charm. The match is about functional relevance, not personality.

As briefly mentioned in Chapter 5, one of the most effective ways to demonstrate functional relevance is through concise, outcome-driven storytelling. Human beings process and retain stories far more readily than credentials or titles. A Fractional Executive who can say, "I've solved this exact problem before," and briefly explains how, creates instant clarity and credibility. These stories compress years of experience into minutes, allowing founders to visualize outcomes rather than interpret resumes. Storytelling is not embellishment; it is translation, turning expertise into evidence the client can recognize and trust.

Some Fractional Executives claim they close an assignment in every interview. That is most likely wishful thinking. Realistically, Fractional Leaders must speak to far more prospects than they will ever engage. Ratios vary widely; some win 1 out of 2, others 1 out of 20. The extremes are rare, with most people landing somewhere in the middle.

Because of that, executives should actively cultivate as many parallel conversations as possible, provided those opportunities meet their criteria. If an opportunity fits but calendar space becomes an issue later, they can negotiate delayed start dates or even hand off to another executive. Once trust and alignment are established, clients are surprisingly flexible.

Disciplined interviewing, clear positioning, and outcome-driven storytelling only matter if the right conversations are happening in the first place. Fractional Executives cannot rely on being "found" at the exact moment a company realizes it needs help. In today's more crowded fractional market, opportunity is created through sustained visibility, not single-point outreach.

As supply has increased and competition has intensified, Fractional Executives must intentionally diversify how opportunities enter their pipeline. The old guidance of relying on one or two primary sources is no longer sufficient. Most successful Fractionals now maintain at least five distinct channels for generating conversations.

These channels typically include:

- **Existing network** nurtured consistently, not activated only when work is needed
- **Network expansion,** especially among professionals who share the same ICP (for example, CROs partnering with CFOs or COOs in the same vertical)

- **Matchmakers** like Vendux, who bring pre-qualified, scoped opportunities
- **Investors** who need trusted operators for their portfolio companies
- **Communities and associations,** industry groups, peer networks, and professional forums where founders already gather

No single channel alone produces a reliable pipeline that holds up over time. Fractional assignments rarely come from a single conversation or outreach moment. Instead, they emerge from repeated exposure across the environments where founders, owners, CEOs, and investors already spend time.

Being "top of mind" is not about constant selling. It is built through consistent presence, relevant contribution, and visible expertise over time. When a founder finally reaches the point of taking action, the executive who feels familiar, credible, and trusted is far more likely to receive the call than the one who simply appears at the moment of need.

Visibility creates the conversation, but scoping determines whether that conversation becomes an engagement.

Once a founder, owner, or CEO reaches out, the Fractional Executive's role shifts quickly from being known to being useful. This is the point where many opportunities are either clarified and advanced or quietly lost. Clear, disciplined scoping turns interest into alignment and protects both parties from mismatched expectations.

Scope begins with the client's desired outcome—where they are today, where they want to go, and what they believe needs to happen in between. Most clients understand their destination but may not know the steps required to get there, especially when the work involves unfamiliar functional areas.

The Fractional Executive must guide the process, ask the right questions, and put the scope into writing. Effective scoping includes:

- Current state
- Target state
- Milestones
- Timeframes
- Expected deliverables
- A realistic evaluation of feasibility

Executives tend to bring enough experience to ground unrealistic goals. For example, if a founder wants revenue growth that defies the underlying sales math, such as funnel size, conversion rates, or sales cycle length, the executive must confidently redirect expectations and recalibrate what success actually looks like.

Once expectations are aligned and feasibility is established, a well-developed scope document can move directly into the contract.

Written, legally sound contracts matter in fractional work, not because they are necessarily complex, but because they often become the point where momentum is either preserved or lost. A well-scoped engagement should translate cleanly into a clear, balanced agreement—one that protects both parties without reopening fundamental questions or slowing the decision process.

In an effective fractional contract, the essentials are explicit and nothing more:

- Scope and goals
- Compensation

- Term and termination
- Independent contractor status
- Core legal protections (confidentiality, intellectual property, indemnification)

Attempts to anticipate every theoretical scenario usually backfire. Overly long or one-sided contracts invite redlines, counterproposals, and extended legal reviews, often creating deal fatigue before the work even begins. Reasonable clients expect fairness, not leverage. When legal terms feel disproportionate to the size and duration of the engagement, trust erodes.

The goal of a fractional contract is not to "win" the negotiation. It is to preserve clarity, signal professionalism, and allow the engagement to begin while energy and alignment are still high. Concise, balanced contracts do exactly that.

The principles behind disciplined scoping and trust-building are easiest to understand when seen in practice. Fractional assignments rarely fail because of a lack of expertise; they falter when expectations are vague, needs are misunderstood, or scope is defined too loosely at the outset. The following case illustrates how a Fractional Executive won an assignment, not by selling aggressively or overpromising outcomes, but by bringing clarity into an uncertain situation and guiding the client toward a well-defined, achievable engagement.

When companies engage Fractional Executives, the success of the assignment is determined long before any work begins. The ability to deliver meaningful outcomes depends on clarity: clarity of need, scope, and expectations on both sides.

In this case, a growth-minded company entered conversations with several potential sales leaders, including full-time candidates, consultants, and Fractional Executives. Leadership knew growth was stalling, but they struggled to articulate why. Revenue targets felt increasingly out of reach, yet the underlying causes were unclear. Like many founders, they could describe symptoms, including missed forecasts, inconsistent pipeline, uneven performance, but not the structural issues beneath them.

The Fractional Sales Executive who ultimately won the assignment did not do so through pure charisma or promises of rapid growth. Instead, they asked disciplined, targeted questions. They probed how deals were sourced, how long the sales cycle actually took, where handoffs broke down, and which constraints could not be changed. They challenged assumptions, recalibrated timelines, and reframed the problem in practical, solvable terms.

Rather than agreeing to a vague mandate to "fix sales," the executive guided the company toward a clearly scoped engagement. Together, they defined the current state, the desired outcomes, and a realistic path between the two. The scope prioritized assessment, focus, and near-term stabilization before pursuing aggressive growth. This clarity created confidence not just in what would be done, but in what would not be attempted prematurely.

Trust developed quickly through evidence. The executive shared relevant examples of having solved very similar problems in comparable environments. They translated experience into concrete scenarios that the founders could recognize. This allowed the company to visualize outcomes rather than rely on hope or credentials.

Once engaged, the Fractional Executive moved deliberately. Early communication was frequent and structured, reinforcing alignment. Quick wins were paired with transparency about constraints and trade-offs. When priorities shifted, as they inevitably do in growth-stage companies, the executive named the changes, documented them, and adjusted scope rather than silently absorbing additional work.

The result was not an instant transformation, but steady progress built on shared understanding. The company gained visibility into its sales reality, leadership regained focus, and expectations stayed aligned throughout the engagement. Just as importantly, the relationship remained healthy because success had been defined realistically from the outset.

This case illustrates a central truth of fractional work: winning the assignment is not about convincing a client to hire you. It is about helping them understand what they actually need and then, together, determining whether the engagement makes sense. The Fractional Executives who succeed are those who bring structure, clarity, and discipline into the sales process itself, long before they ever begin executing the work.

Once an assignment begins, the first 30, maybe 60 days, determine whether a Fractional Executive is viewed as a trusted leader or merely an external advisor. Early execution sets the tone for authority, momentum, and long-term impact.

Trust is not something an executive can literally build. It develops and grows for the CEO as they confirm through evidence that the Fractional Executive understands them, understands the business, and can deliver outcomes. The early days are where this confirmation happens. Clarity, disciplined execution, and visible progress in this phase establish authority faster than any resume or reputation ever could.

Trust grows when executives:

- Ask excellent, targeted questions
- Understand what the CEO values most (numbers, people, operations, speed, etc.)
- Provide tangible, credible, scenario-specific plans
- Demonstrate they have solved this exact problem before
- Show they can execute, not just advise

Fractional Executives often share preliminary 30/60/90-day frameworks before contracts are signed. These frameworks are not promises; they are working hypotheses that demonstrate structured thinking, realistic sequencing, and an understanding of trade-offs. This level of specificity differentiates true expertise from general claims like "I can do that."

Some Executives worry they are "giving too much away" during this pre-contract phase. But most CEOs would not be able to execute the plan themselves because they lack the time, capacity, and functional depth. Sharing these specifics establishes the credibility necessary to get the contract across the finish line.

But even with strong early momentum, no fractional engagement unfolds exactly as planned. In startup and scale-up environments, priorities shift frequently. Product timelines move, funding assumptions change, and new information surfaces. Fractional Executives must expect this and plan for it, rather than treat change as a failure of scoping. How an executive handles inevitable change determines whether this early trust compounds or erodes.

Consistent communication is the primary mechanism for managing scope creep. Executives should regularly share what they are working on, what is coming next, and what trade-offs are emerging.

Early, transparent communication allows for:

- Adjusting priorities without panic
- Reframing timelines before trust erodes
- Avoiding misalignment between effort and expectation
- Determining when contract amendments are required

Highly rigid contracts can complicate those necessary changes. Fractional work benefits from structured flexibility: a clearly defined near-term plan (often 30/60/90-day), paired with openness beyond that horizon. This balance preserves accountability without locking the engagement into assumptions that no longer reflect reality.

In some cases, the most effective way to structure a fractional engagement is to begin with a paid assessment phase rather than a long-term commitment. These assessments typically run for 30 to 45 days and are formalized under contract, with clear scope, deliverables, and decision points.

During this period, the executive works within the organization to understand the context from the inside, validate assumptions, and build a detailed execution plan. While many executives who lead assessments are ultimately selected to carry the work forward, continuation is not guaranteed. Even so, the trust and clarity built during a strong assessment often position the executive as the natural choice for the fractional engagement.

Delivering Results as a Fractional Executive:

Winning the assignment is only the beginning. Once a Fractional Executive is inside the business, the dynamics shift from selling and scoping to execution, communication, and expectation management. Fractional engagements almost always begin on a high note—the founder, owner, or CEO is excited to finally have senior-level help, and the executive arrives with fresh energy and immediate expertise. But the mistake many new Fractionals make is assuming that this early momentum will last throughout a six- or nine-month engagement. It will not.

What determines whether an engagement sustains momentum or quietly unravels comes down to a small set of execution principles.

The biggest and most common pitfall is a lack of communication. The responsibility for maintaining communication lies primarily with the Fractional Executive, not the client. Fractionals move in and out of assignments constantly; they are the service provider and the experienced party in the fractional engagement, and therefore, they must own communication.

Regular updates should address:

- What was done
- What is being worked on next
- What outcomes were achieved
- What adjustments are needed

- What decisions the CEO needs to make

This avoids surprises, prevents drift, and allows the CEO to redirect if priorities change. Communication protects the executive as much as it supports the client.

Contrary to what many believe, Fractional Executives often encounter less resistance from coworkers than an equivalent full-time leader would, because Fractionals are:

- In the organization temporarily,
- focused on a limited scope,
- not competing for promotions,
- often far more experienced than those they lead,
- and not a threat to anyone's long-term career.

As a result, friction is less common than in full-time leadership transitions. Issues can arise, but most stem from ordinary human dynamics, and most are solvable. The primary relationship the fractional must always actively manage is with the CEO, founder, or owner.

Once execution is underway, one of the fastest ways a fractional engagement derails is through unmanaged scope creep.

Scope creep is almost inevitable, but it only becomes a problem when it goes unacknowledged. The fractional must:

- Name it immediately ("This is outside the original scope.")
- Document it in weekly updates
- Ask what should be removed, reprioritized, or extended
- If necessary, suggest changes to the contract

Because in this situation, something has to give: either the timeline, the budget, or the workload. Fractionals get into trouble when they absorb scope creep silently and try to "just get it done." That leads to missed goals, diluted impact, and eventually damaged credibility.

Over-promising is another trap, especially for new Fractionals eager to win the engagement.

Executives must avoid:

- Agreeing to unrealistic timelines
- Accepting scopes requiring impossible hours
- Promising outcomes before understanding the details
- Taking responsibility for goals they cannot influence

Early conversations between the Executive and the founder, owner, or CEO offer the perfect moment to set expectations, challenge unrealistic goals, and reframe timelines. Most founders know very little about fractional work. They are often relieved when an executive brings reality, structure, and clarity.

Fractionals must never commit to delivering in eight hours something that takes twenty. Over-promising always backfires.

Even when scope and expectations are discussed openly, another hidden risk often surfaces: unclear metrics.

Many founders cannot articulate their metrics because they've never analyzed their data in that way. Some examples include:

- They know they closed 10 customers,
- but don't know the average length of the sales cycle,
- or the average deal size,
- or the repeatability of the process,
- or even their real **budget constraints**.

Founders often respond with anecdotes ("Some closed in two weeks, some in two years"), rather than data-driven averages. Fractional Executives must ask the right questions, break down the data, and provide clarity that the founder lacks.

This is especially true at smaller companies, where founders are product experts, not business experts, and often wear hats they shouldn't.

Most fractional engagements end successfully once the goals are achieved. Of those who do not, not all end due to execution failures; as outlined above some end because the business itself can no longer sustain the work, when the client simply runs out of money. This is especially common among early-stage startups and small businesses with volatile cash flow. When that happens:

- The business loses the benefit of the investment already made.
- The executive loses projected months of income.
- The work is left unfinished, often right before the payoff can begin.

It's rarely malicious. Most founders simply miscalculate how long it will take to see results or how quickly their cash will burn. But it is a real-life pitfall of fractional work. Some financing mechanisms exist for go-to-market investments[15], but they do not eliminate the risk entirely.

Understanding the financial runway is about protecting both the executive's livelihood and the integrity of the engagement.

The Fractional Executives who succeed long-term are not the ones who win the most assignments, but the ones who consistently choose the right ones and manage them with discipline from start to finish.

---

[15] https://www.vendux.org/financing

CHAPTER 7

Sustaining Success as a Fractional Leader

In the early phase of fractional work, opportunities can come fast. What matters, though, is not how quickly you can land the first assignment, but whether you can sustain an impactful delivery across many. Long-term success as a Fractional Executive is built on repeatability. The executives who sustain this career for years are not necessarily the most talented strategists. They are the ones who manage multiple clients without diluting impact, protect their time through disciplined boundaries, stay relevant as markets evolve, and build a durable ecosystem around their work.

As Dr. GSK Velu put it, "The power of small steps in any entrepreneur journey brings an understanding of and confidence in the ability to adapt, analyze, solve problems, make improvements, grow, and see the difference at a remarkable level."[16] Fractional success is exactly that: small steps taken consistently across client management, operations, learning, and positioning until the work becomes stable, predictable, and sustainable.

Managing Multiple Clients Without Dilution of Impact

A fractional business only works when the assignments stay fractional. The easiest way to lose trust, quietly and without any dramatic failure, is to be spread too thin. When that happens, results weaken,

---

[16] https://www.linkedin.com/pulse/importance-small-steps-success-journey-dr-g-s-k-velu/

communication slips, and the executive starts doing unpaid hours just to keep up. Clients may not say it directly, but they feel it. The engagement becomes reactive instead of intentional. The executive becomes "available" instead of impactful.

The solution is not working harder. It's managing the client mix and all related calendars with discipline.

A "key client" is a customer who is considered highly valuable to a company, typically generating a substantial portion of its revenue, significantly impacting its brand image, and requiring a dedicated level of attention and strategic partnership to maintain the business. Fractional Leaders have key clients, too. And the reality is simple: a fractional practice can support multiple clients, but it cannot support multiple key clients at the same time unless the hours, scopes, and expectations are explicitly designed for that reality.

This is why, as a Fractional Executive, your calendar is your most valuable asset. It is the only resource you cannot replenish, and it is also the clearest indicator of your business's sustainability.

Time Management:
The Big Rocks, Small Rocks, and Sand

One of the most useful productivity metaphors for fractional work is the "big rocks, small rocks, and sand" framework. Imagine your time as a glass jar. Into that jar, you have to fit everything required to deliver across multiple clients while still maintaining your own business.

The big rocks are your highest-impact priorities: the work that defines your value and produces outcomes clients can feel. For a Fractional Executive, big rocks often include strategic planning sessions, leadership alignment meetings, key client reviews, and milestone delivery, especially for any client consuming 50% or more of your weekly capacity.

The small rocks are important supporting tasks: internal status updates, review meetings, follow-ups, deck preparation, dashboard review, and decision-making moments that keep momentum moving. These tasks matter, but they exist to support the big rocks.

The sand is everything else: emails, scheduling, ad hoc requests, Slack messages, quick calls that "should only take five minutes," and the daily noise that expands to fill whatever space you give it.

If you start by filling the jar with sand, there will be no room left for the rocks. But when you place the big rocks first, the smaller rocks and sand can fit around them. This is not a motivational idea. It is an operational reality.

Practically, this means beginning each week by identifying the two or three big rocks that must be delivered to maintain credibility across your client portfolio. Those are your non-negotiables. You block time for them first. Then you place small rocks around them. And you contain the sand in fixed windows because if you don't, it will fill the entire rest of the jar.

This same framework applies to how you structure your client portfolio. Many successful Fractionals intentionally design a mix: one big rock as the key client, maybe requiring 40-50% of your time. Then you place one, maybe two smaller rocks into the jar, clients that need 8-10 hours a week, plus maybe another small rock of advisory work. And the sand is those activities you need to do in order to run your business. This mix creates stable income, diversified risk, and enough capacity to deliver excellence without burning out.

Boundaries:
A Professional Obligation, not a Personal Preference

Fractional Leaders often struggle with boundaries because boundaries can feel like refusal. But in fractional work, boundaries are not a personality trait. They are part of the service model.

If you support multiple clients, your availability must be structured rather than improvised. That means explicitly defining days of availability, hours for certain activities, response-time expectations, and communication channels (text vs. email vs. calls). It means limits on weekend work. And it means reinforcing, without apology: "I support multiple clients. This is how I protect everyone's results."

Founders, owners, and CEOs will often test boundaries, unintentionally. Many work 60 to 80 hours per week and assume everyone around them works the same way. A Fractional Executive must correct this assumption immediately and consistently. Not with defensiveness, but with clarity: what you can do, when you can do it, and what the response process looks like.

Boundaries become especially critical when the role requires high responsiveness, when the company claims 24/7 availability externally, or when the workload begins exceeding the agreed-upon hours. Some roles simply cannot be fractionalized. An important part of early due diligence is determining whether the function is structurally compatible with part-time leadership.

Dilution of Impact:
When Fractional Is No Longer Enough

Even when an engagement begins cleanly, roles evolve. Businesses grow. Priorities shift. The scope expands. And at some point, the work can outgrow the fractional model.

When a fractional role becomes too large for part-time capacity, the executive must name it. Early. Clearly. And professionally:

"This is no longer a fractional role. You need either a full-time leader or a different structure."

This is one of the most important sentences a Fractional Executive learns to say. It protects the client from disappointment and protects the executive from slow credibility erosion.

The CEO is the one who must determine what matters most, the short list of tasks the fractional should focus on, a short list of high-priority items, and not the laundry list of A through Z. Concentrated impact beats diluted effort every time. The more senior you are, the more you must resist becoming the "catch-all." Fractional Leaders win by narrowing focus, not expanding it.

When Matches Fail

Despite careful vetting, some engagements simply don't work. The reasons are rarely dramatic. They're usually structural or interpersonal realities that only become visible once execution begins: misaligned working styles, resource constraints, misrepresented data, unclear decision-making authority, shifting priorities, or incompatibilities that weren't apparent during the matching process.

When a match fails mid-engagement, the client often places the executive and—if applicable—the agency that facilitated the engagement in the same bucket. That is one reason disciplined qualification and strong early communication matter so much. It's also why experienced Fractionals treat fit as a real business variable, not a "soft" factor.

The goal is not necessarily perfection. The goal is professionalism: naming misalignment early, documenting it clearly, and exiting cleanly when necessary.

Continuous Learning: Staying Relevant as the Market Evolves

Longevity as a Fractional Executive has two layers. First: Can the model be sustained long-term? Yes. Many executives have already done it for a decade or more. Some started before the term "fractional" was popular, simply by building portfolios and delivering outcomes. Second, how do you sustain demand as the market evolves? That is the harder question, and the answer is continuous relevance.

Fractional work does not come with a company training budget. No one mandates development. The market does. Tools, platforms, buyer expectations, and operating norms shift quickly, especially in go-to-market functions. If you are doing fractional work the same way today as you did your full-time job five or ten years ago, you are falling behind.

Staying current is not about chasing trends. It's about maintaining fluency: understanding modern tool ecosystems, staying sharp on what founders are doing now, and refining your playbooks so they remain effective in today's environment. Your credibility is tied to outcomes. Outcomes are tied to the current reality. Continuous learning is how you keep that link intact.

Building Community with Other Fractional Leaders

Fractional work is independent, but it should not be isolated. One of the most consistent patterns among long-tenured Fractionals is community: peer relationships, cohort networks, informal advisory circles, matchmaker relationships, and trusted operator groups.

Community does more than provide support. It increases deal flow, improves judgment, strengthens pattern recognition, and provides a feedback loop that keeps you sharp. It also creates optionality: the ability to refer work out, bring others in, collaborate on delivery, and avoid taking poor-fit engagements out of fear.

A fractional practice becomes more stable when it is connected to other capable people. Isolation increases volatility. Network decreases it.

Scaling Options: Staying Solo, Subcontracting, or Building a Boutique Practice

Not every Fractional Executive wants to scale. Many prefer staying solo: a small portfolio, strong income, high flexibility, and control over time. That is a valid model, and for many, it is the point of being a Fractional.

But fractional work can also evolve into a business with leverage. Typically, executives choose one of three paths.

The first is subcontracting execution work. Many Fractionals begin outsourcing lower-level tasks, especially in marketing, finance, and operational administration, to remain focused on strategy and leadership. This might include marketing copy, design, ad execution, business development work, accounting, or controller-level work. Subcontracting doesn't necessarily turn you into an agency. It simply protects your valuable time and expertise and increases capacity.

The second path is building a boutique firm. This is a larger step: building a team around yourself, becoming the lead strategist and face of the firm while others handle execution and client management. Some Fractionals love this model. Others find it pulls them away from the work they enjoy most. Either way, it's a conscious choice that requires a different operating mindset.

The third option is productized services. Many experienced Fractionals create repeatable offerings: audits, assessments, playbooks, process builds, frameworks. Productization increases scalability and speeds up delivery. It also reduces sales friction because clients understand what they are buying. A clear, productized offer can also serve as a feeder into higher-value retainer work.

Scaling is not required. But optionality matters. The longer you stay in fractional work, the more valuable it becomes to have multiple ways to generate income without always trading hours for revenue.

Longevity: Keeping Demand Strong Over Time

The most common reason executives return to full-time employment is not for the benefits. It is to get out of a state of constant volatility. Fractional work requires continually generating engagements, tolerating uncertain income, and managing fluctuating utilization. When someone cannot maintain enough work and feels persistent stress from unpredictability, that is usually what drives them back to a corporate role.

The antidote is not hope. It's structure.

First, your rates must reflect reality. Benefits, taxes, downtime, business development time, continuing education, and non-billable work must be priced in. You cannot simply fractionalize your corporate take-home salary. Healthcare alone can range from hundreds to thousands per month without employer coverage. Many executives use a cash compensation multiplier as a starting point, but true sustainability often requires more than a simple conversion. A fractional practice must fund the entire system around it, not just the billable hours.

Second, demand is protected through specialization. As the fractional landscape becomes more crowded, generalists blend in. Specialists stand out. They don't win by appealing to everyone; they win by becoming indispensable to a specific type of client facing a specific set of problems.

When fractional work first gained traction, many executives relied on their breadth of experience. After decades as versatile operators, CMOs who could also speak to sales, CFOs who had handled HR, and CROs who had worn product hats, offering a wide range of capabilities felt logical. More skills should mean more opportunities.

In practice, the opposite often happens. Generalists blend into a crowded market of similar resumes and vague positioning. Without a clear differentiator, it becomes difficult to create urgency or relevance. Clients facing a defined problem aren't looking for someone who can do everything; they want someone who has repeatedly solved their specific problem with measurable results.

Specialist Fractionals operate differently. Their positioning is focused, their messaging clear, and their value proposition easy to understand. Whether it's "I help SaaS companies scale from $1M to $10M ARR" or "I work with private equity-backed manufacturers post-acquisition," clarity allows clients to recognize fit immediately. This focus shortens sales cycles, sharpens referrals, and aligns opportunities before conversations even begin.

The market reinforces this pattern. The most in-demand Fractional Leaders tend to concentrate on a small number of adjacent verticals, company stages, or go-to-market models. Matchmakers and platforms no longer search for "seasoned executives" in general terms; they look for precise expertise such as "healthcare revenue operations," "multi-site retail growth," or "compliance-driven SaaS finance." Riches are in niches.

Niche does not mean small. It means intentional. A niche can be defined by industry, company stage, problem type, buyer persona, technology stack, or transformation scenario. **The key is choosing where you have driven repeatable success and where your experience compounds rather than stretches.**

Third, longevity requires pacing. Fractional work is often the final major chapter of an executive career, the third phase. The model provides exceptional control: you can scale up or down based on lifestyle, season, or health. But it should not be framed as semi-retirement. Fractional Leadership is real leadership responsibility. Sustaining demand requires staying engaged, adaptable, and up to date.

And staying current is critical. Fractional Executives must commit to continuous education. No one mandates this except the market. Technology is evolving too quickly to remain effective while relying on tools and playbooks that are even just five years old. When I began my sales career, the only tool I needed to think about was the Customer Relationship Management (CRM). Today, an entire ecosystem of sales technology exists and a combination of several tools is part of a successful tech stack. A Fractional Sales Leader must know how to navigate them all. Executives must invest time in learning new tools, AI-driven systems, and emerging platforms to remain competitive.

Finally, longevity requires judgment. Not every client is worth having. Not every engagement is sustainable. The long-term Fractionals are not just good at delivery; they are good at selection. They protect their time, energy, and reputation by designing a practice that can actually be carried out over the years.

A Fractional Executive entered the model with strong credentials and immediate demand. Within weeks of announcing availability, he had accepted the first five clients. Each engagement, taken individually, seemed reasonable. Together, they created an unworkable structure.

Two of the clients required rapid turnaround and high responsiveness. One was underfunded but ambitious, with expectations that outpaced reality. Another was still defining its problem and relied on the executive for constant direction. None of the scopes were clearly wrong, but none were tightly bounded either.

At first, the executive absorbed the pressure quietly. He worked evenings to stay ahead, responded quickly to maintain goodwill, and reassured himself that the intensity would ease once things stabilized. They never did.

The earliest warning signs were subtle. Weekly updates became less structured. Strategic conversations drifted into tactical firefighting. One client began escalating requests outside of agreed-upon hours, assuming availability rather than asking for it. Instead of resetting expectations, the executive accommodated the behavior, worried that pushing back might jeopardize the relationship.

As utilization crept upward, impact declined. Decisions slowed. Follow-through weakened. Clients sensed the shift not as failure, but as inconsistency. One engagement ended abruptly when results fell short of expectations. Another reduced hours quietly. Revenue fell, but workload didn't.

Sustaining success as a Fractional Executive is not one decision. It is a series of small, consistent steps: protecting calendar integrity, maintaining boundaries, keeping skills current, staying connected to peers, choosing the right scaling path, and building a model that can withstand market shifts. Do that, and fractional work becomes what it is meant to be: not a temporary escape from corporate life, but a durable, high-control, high-impact way to finish a career on your own terms.

PART III

The SMB Leader's Guide to Fractional Talent

CHAPTER 8

Why Fractional?

Most founders, owners, and CEOs don't look for "Fractional Leadership" as a concept or to fill a seat on the org chart. They are searching for a solution because sales have stalled, cash is tightening, execution is slipping, or the team has outgrown the systems holding it together. The fractional model matters for one reason: it lets you add senior capability in the exact increment you need, when you need it, without forcing an all-or-nothing hiring decision. This chapter explains why that matters, when it works, and how founders, owners, and CEOs should think about fractional talent as a strategic growth lever, not a temporary workaround.

From the CEO's vantage point, Fractional Leadership is fundamentally about solving problems. They see challenges across sales, marketing, operations, finance, product, growth, or fundraising. They need a specialist. The essential question becomes: Do I need this skill set full-time? And in many cases, especially in smaller companies, the answer is no.

And so, instead of forcing one person into multiple unrelated roles or promoting someone internally beyond their capabilities, the CEO can fractionalize the need and bring in the exact expertise required for the exact amount of time. This avoids compromises, handoffs, and inefficiencies.

Fractional Is Leadership, not "Advice-Only"

Some CEOs need help understanding that fractional is not "consulting" or "advice-only." It's real leadership responsibility. Yet there are persistent misconceptions: concerns about loyalty, confidentiality, commitment, or the idea that 10 hours per week isn't enough.

These prejudices can be countered with structure, clarity, and data. Studies and workplace research repeatedly show that commitment, performance, and trustworthiness are not determined by employment classification[17]. And as with any leadership role, trust is built through clarity, communication, and accountability, rather than on whether someone is W-2 or 1099.

Fractional Executives can and should list the multiple engagements they hold simultaneously on LinkedIn. In fact, it often benefits both the company and the executive. When investors or customers view a company's LinkedIn profile and see one or more fractional C-suite Executives (CXOs) listed, it strengthens credibility. The same is true in pitch decks, where founders want to show they've covered essential functional areas without hiring full-time staff before they can afford to. Fractional Leadership fills that need.

Fractional Executives as Levers: Growth, Transformation, Stabilization

Fractional Executives serve as powerful levers for CEOs, enabling growth, transformation, and stabilization.

Growth comes from solving talent gaps early, accelerating momentum, and right-sizing roles so a founder, owner, or CEO can scale more quickly. Hiring one full-time executive gives you just one skill set; hiring three Fractional Executives gives you three specialized skill sets at roughly the same combined cost.

---

[17] https://blogs.vorecol.com/blog-how-do-performance-metrics-differ-between-contractors-and-fulltime-employees-127052

Transformation is a requirement when a company reaches a plateau and needs someone who has successfully navigated the next phase of its growth. Someone who has already led an organization through the next level and who doesn't need a learning curve. They can see immediately what needs to change.

Stabilization often needs to happen when growth has been so rapid that operational structures can't keep up. The wheels feel like they're coming off. A Fractional Executive who has already operated at the next level can step in, steady the system, and build the structure needed for sustainable scale without slowing momentum.

Fractional Leadership is far more common than many realize. Some startups present a fully staffed executive team on their website or pitch deck, but in reality, all those roles are fractional. Founders may have multiple Fractional Executives working as CFO, CMO, COO, and CRO, while the founders themselves still hold full-time roles elsewhere. Fractionalizing gives early-stage companies access to capabilities they could never afford otherwise.

Fractional Leadership is not a stopgap; it's a strategic advantage.

When the Going Gets Tough, Go Fractional

The state of the fractional industry is often a topic of discussion, and that includes the details of what is happening on the supply and demand side. As an industry, we need to tell the story.

On the supply side, those of us who have been in this space for a while are currently seeing an influx of talent, maybe even a temporary oversupply. Companies jumping on the bandwagon of layoffs and the post-pandemic return to business as usual in the corporate world have many executives looking for alternatives.

Most Fractional Executives are experienced and highly qualified with the skills and abilities to deliver an immediate and lasting impact. They thrive on variety, delivering value, and managing complex organizational challenges and situations requiring change. They end up choosing a career in fractional work; they choose independent employment in the growing gig economy.

Being a Fractional requires additional talents, including stick-to-itiveness, determination, and the long-term vision to build a business. For the most part, it is not a short-term fix or a temporary plug with instant gratification.

The demand side of fractional work is continually growing. Recent, current, and future disruptions to business as usual will highlight the benefits of Fractional Executives again and again, thereby proliferating the role.

A History of Growth

While some Fractional Executives were already active prior to 2019, the pandemic in 2020 led to greater acceptance of remote and part-time work, thereby sparking the growth we are seeing today.

The pandemic was a fundamentally new experience for all companies, and as restrictions shut down business as usual, companies responded with several strategies, some that worked and others that did not; some that were new and innovative, and others that reflected the tried-and-true:

- Layoffs
- Hiring freezes
- Work from home
- Taxpayer-funded support programs

- Furloughs
- and … contracting

Once the initial shock of the previously unknown had passed, contracting the necessary skills, especially on a fractional basis, provided an alternative to traditional hiring.

Post-pandemic, a skilled talent shortage was ever-present. Rand Europe estimated that the shortage of skilled workers in digital industries will cost the 14 largest economies in the G20 a staggering $11.5 trillion in lost GDP growth by 2030[18].

And when demand was high and the skilled labor market was tight, Fractional Executives provided an additional talent pool that companies tapped into.

Some of those more innovative ideas used during the pandemic provide a blueprint for navigating the current and any future economic uncertainty. Because the often indiscriminate action of layoffs deprives companies of much-needed talent, especially when that talent is now necessary to:

- Make the product portfolio recession-proof
- Identify and implement additional channels to market
- Lead a sales-driven turnaround
- Enter new markets to spark new growth
- and so many more steps that help companies navigate choppy economic waters

Fractional is the alternative to all-or-nothing. Fractional Executives bring much-needed talent at less than the cost of a full-time hire. They

---

[18]https://www.rand.org/content/dam/rand/pubs/research_reports/RRA1500/RRA1533-1/RAND_RRA1533-1.pdf

are the perfect alternative, the one that can get a company out from between a rock and a hard place.

And so the future for Fractional Executive work is bright. Regardless of the economy, fractionalizing work at the executive level enables a different growth model. Instead of staffing up in large steps, the necessary talent and skills can be added sooner and in the right increments. CEOs do not have to wait until they can afford the full cost of an executive.

And the result of taking smaller steps is not just equal; it often leads to faster growth:

- The right skills are in place just when you need them, not when you can afford them.
- There is no loss in productivity due to multitasking or suboptimal talent.
- At any time, the skills can be right-sized for the needs of the business.

Overall, the future of talent management, and with it, the success of companies, will hinge on the ability to be more tactical and selective.

Why Choose Fractional Services Over Full-Time Hires

Staffing up, especially at the executive level, has traditionally meant hiring full-time. The timing of that decision was almost always driven by affordability: could the company carry the fully loaded cost of someone with the experience, tenure, and relationships required to succeed? As a result, executive teams started small, grew slowly, and each leader wore multiple hats. In the startup world, this is often celebrated as scrappy and lean.

The reality is less romantic. The more hats an executive wears, the greater the strain and the higher the likelihood of performance gaps. No matter how capable or hardworking someone is, being overtasked forces trade-offs. One function improves while others quietly deteriorate. And when leadership is constantly firefighting, strategy becomes an afterthought.

This is where Fractional Executives become a structurally better alternative. Fractionalizing work allows organizations to contract the precise amount of talent needed for each task, strategic leadership, process design, coaching, or execution, without forcing one person to take on the impossible role of covering multiple areas of responsibility. Complex work is broken into manageable components and assigned to specialists. The result is better outcomes and faster progress. Specialization improves quality. Focus improves speed.

Before comparing Fractional to full-time, it's critical to understand what a Fractional Executive actually does. These are seasoned leaders who step in to solve specific problems, lead critical initiatives, implement new strategies, or guide organizations through transitions. Their value is not tied to hours worked, but to outcomes delivered. Even on a part-time basis, their experience often makes them indispensable.

Understanding the role also means looking way beyond a title. A successful fractional engagement starts by defining what must be achieved and what work must be executed, typically within the first three to six months. Clarity around whether the role is primarily strategic or tactical is essential. It determines not only who you hire, but how you structure and compensate the engagement.

One of the primary reasons companies turn to Fractional Executives is access to specialized expertise without the long-term commitment of a full-time employee. Fractional Executives typically command rates ranging from $150 to $400 per hour, depending on their expertise and seniority, as well as the complexity of the assignment. Whether pricing is hourly, retainer-based, or outcome-driven, the math matters, especially when the alternative is a full-time executive with salary, benefits, bonuses, taxes, recruiting costs, and ramp time.

The starting point is an honest assessment of need:

- What is the scope and complexity of the work that requires executive-level expertise?
- How long is that expertise required: a defined project or an ongoing role?
- How much of that expertise is truly required to achieve the desired outcomes?
- What impact will successful execution have on the business?
- What budget needs to be allocated to this initiative?

Answering these questions allows companies to right-size the role and the investment. Industry benchmarks for comparable full-time executives provide a baseline. Fractional Executives often command a premium not because they are more expensive, but because they bring depth, speed, and flexibility without long-term overhead.

Staffing in large increments is an outdated growth model. In nearly every other area of life, we already understand the power of small, deliberate steps: Kaizen[19], compounding, personal development, and wealth-building all rely on incremental progress. Fractionalizing executive work applies the same principle to leadership.

The result is not equivalent growth; it is often faster growth at a reduced investment:

- The right skills are in place when they are needed, not when they are finally affordable.

---

[19] https://kaizen.com/what-is-kaizen/

- Productivity improves because leaders focus on what they do best.
- Capability can be expanded or reduced quickly as business needs evolve.

This is why contracting executives on a part-time or project basis has become such an attractive alternative.

Cost efficiency is an obvious driver. Hiring a full-time executive in areas such as sales, marketing, operations, technology, or finance is expensive, once salary, benefits, and overhead are included. Fractional services provide access to top-tier talent while allowing the often-scarce capital to be allocated where it creates the greatest return.

Flexibility and scalability matter just as much. Business needs shift with growth stage, market conditions, and strategic priorities. Full-time hires create fixed, long-term commitments. Fractional engagements allow companies to scale leadership up or down as needed, preserving agility.

Specialized expertise is another advantage. Many small- and medium-sized companies need executive-level guidance but cannot justify hiring specialists full-time. Fractional Executives bring niche experience and pattern recognition that would otherwise be inaccessible. A Fractional GTM Leader, for example, can quickly assess the current state, design a system, and begin execution without months of onboarding.

Speed to impact is often decisive. Fractional Executives are experienced operators. They diagnose faster, decide faster, and execute faster, an advantage when momentum matters.

Risk reduction is the final piece. Full-time hiring carries real risk: misalignment, underperformance, or being stuck with a fixed asset in times of changing business needs. Fractional engagements allow companies to test fit and impact. If the work is successful, the engagement can continue. If not, the company can pivot without long-term consequences.

While the upfront investment may appear significant, the Return on Investment (ROI) must be evaluated in context. Data consistently shows that Fractional Leadership deployed against critical problems delivers meaningful bottom-line impact. In mission-critical situations, investing in a highly experienced executive often reduces risk rather than increases it.

There is also room for flexibility in the structure of fractional engagements. Rates may vary based on duration, scope, or stage of the engagement. Some roles, particularly in sales, may include variable compensation or success-based components to further de-risk the investment. In certain cases, equity may be part of the conversation. These decisions should be made deliberately, with alignment on expectations from the outset.

Choosing Fractional Leadership is not about cutting corners. It is about precision. When needs are clearly defined and expertise is properly matched, Fractional Executives deliver outsized value. For many organizations, this approach produces better outcomes, faster progress, and a more sustainable path to growth than traditional full-time hiring ever could.

The Commitment Question: Are Fractionals "Less Invested"?

Every so often, a founder will say:

"I'm not completely comfortable bringing an outside, non-committed, part-time person to figure our process out at this stage."

My instinctive response is always the same: Fractional Executives are often more committed than their full-time counterpart because their future work relies on reputation, referrals, and a successful track record. They are paid on the understanding of goals and objectives being delivered, not merely on attendance.

SHRM defines employee engagement and commitment as the level of satisfaction and pride employees have in their work and employer, their belief in the significance of their job, and the perception that their contributions are valued[20]. And as freelance and gig work grows, external workers are becoming critical to organizations. They drive innovation, meet operational demands, and execute strategy. They should be considered an essential workforce segment, not a secondary one.

Empirical evidence has not supported the expectation of lower commitment among temporary workers. Studies have found that temporary workers can exhibit similar or even higher levels of commitment. Temporary work can shift the bond from long-term "organizational loyalty" to a performance-driven bond centered on reputation, outcomes, referrals, and future assignments[21].

In the case of Fractional Executives, experienced professionals who have already held senior leadership roles before, often for decades, the concern about commitment is usually misplaced. Their reputation is essential. Their performance is visible. And they understand the impact of their presence and departure.

---

[20] https://www.shrm.org/topics-tools/news/employee-relations/what-why-employee-engagement
[21] https://www.researchgate.net/publication/242022193_The_psychological_contract_organisational_commitment_and_job_satisfaction_of_temporary_staff

As a result, it can be framed as: Contracted Fractional Executives tend to be more committed and engaged than many of their permanent peers for several reasons:

1. Their reputation is crucial for securing future assignments.
2. They are highly interested in expanding their network and obtaining referrals.
3. In some cases, it functions as try-before-you-buy, where performance can lead to permanence.

Confidentiality and Trust: Employee vs. Contractor

Another concern often brought up is access to sensitive business information. Founders, owners, and CEOs sometimes prefer a fully employed CXO over a part-time contractor because they assume the contractor is inherently riskier.

The more accurate frame is that risk exists with both employees and contractors. The meaningful question is whether your agreements and practices are sound.

The growing role of Non-Disclosure Agreements (NDA) is part of the broader reality: confidentiality is protected by enforceable agreements, clear definitions, and consistent onboarding/offboarding protocols. Contractors are not exempt. A properly structured service agreement should mirror the substance of an NDA: clear definitions of confidential information, explicit expectations, ownership of work product and intellectual property (IP), return/destruction of materials, and survival clauses after termination.

Sales roles are a special case because sales leaders sit closest to customer relationships, pricing, contracts, and competitive positioning. That proximity increases the need for strong confidentiality clauses and clean exit protocols, regardless of whether the person is an employee or a contractor.

Should a non-compete clause apply to a Fractional Executive?

The answer, predictably, is "it depends." More precisely, it depends on whose interests are being weighed, how the clause is written, and where in the United States and the world the parties operate.

From a company's standpoint, the impulse to include a non-compete is understandable. Fractional Executives often gain deep access to strategy, pricing, vendor relationships, and future roadmap decisions. In competitive markets, founders and boards worry—sometimes rightly— that this knowledge could be leveraged by a rival.

However, many companies overreach by transplanting full-time employee non-competes into a contractor agreement. Broad language restricting work across an entire industry, long post-engagement "cooling-off" periods, or vague definitions of "competitor" can backfire. Such clauses may be unenforceable, delay contract execution, or discourage top-tier fractional talent from engaging at all.

Fractional Executives operate differently from traditional employees. Their value proposition is built on working with multiple clients—often within the same general domain—while maintaining strict confidentiality boundaries.

A broad non-compete can effectively shut down a Fractional Executive's business. If "corporate gifting," "SaaS," or "construction" is defined expansively, the restriction may prevent the executive from earning a living in their established niche. From the executive's perspective, this is not a minor inconvenience; it strikes at the core of their professional model.

Legally, non-competes are increasingly on shaky ground in the U.S. Enforceability varies by state, but the overall trend is clear: restrictions are narrowing, not expanding.

California is currently the most definitive example. With limited exceptions, post-termination non-competes are void under state law, regardless of whether the worker is an employee or an independent contractor. A non-compete in a California-based 1099 agreement is likely unenforceable, no matter how carefully drafted.

Other states allow non-competes but require they be reasonable in scope, duration, and geography, and tied to a legitimate business interest. Importantly, courts often scrutinize non-competes in contractor agreements more closely than those in employment contracts, precisely because contractors are presumed to operate independent businesses.

For most companies working with Fractional Executives, the best solution is not a traditional non-compete. Instead:

- Define and strengthen confidentiality and IP ownership clauses
- Prohibit work with a short, clearly named list of direct competitors during the active engagement only
- Avoid post-termination restrictions, particularly in restrictive states
- Be explicit about what constitutes a conflict of interest

This approach aligns incentives, respects legal boundaries, and reflects the realities of Fractional Leadership.

Fractional Executive vs. Consultant: Which One Do You Need?

Many companies turn to outsourced expertise, but two options are often conflated: the Fractional Executive and the consultant. Both can create value, but they serve different needs.

A Fractional Executive provides broad strategic oversight and leadership. They function as part of the executive team. They shape the strategy, align the function with business goals, build the system, and drive execution through the team. They are accountable for outcomes.

A consultant typically focuses on narrower problem-solving: process analysis, training, funnel improvements, market insights, and short-term deliverables. Consultants advise and recommend. Fractional Executives lead, build, and operate.

The decision comes down to what the business actually needs:

- If you need leadership, direction, and accountability, you need a Fractional Executive.
- If you need targeted recommendations or tactical support on a narrow issue, a consultant may be sufficient.

This distinction matters because it clarifies expectations. A mismatch here is one of the most common reasons engagements disappoint: the company hires a consultant when it really needs leadership, or it hires a Fractional Executive and expects "hands-on implementation" without providing authority, access, or integration.

Why Fractional Works

Fractional Leadership gives founders, owners, and CEOs a practical alternative to the old all-or-nothing model. It allows a business to solve real problems earlier, right-size talent, reduce risk, accelerate execution, and build credibility without waiting until a full-time executive is affordable or structurally justified.

For small business owners, the value is straightforward: fractional talent is the mechanism that lets you add the right skill at the right time in the right increment. You don't have to staff the future all at once. You can deliberately, intelligently, and with far less waste build it in steps.

And once you understand that fractional is not a compromise, but a model built for agility, specialization, and speed, the next question naturally becomes: how do you choose the right Fractional Leader, structure the engagement, and set it up for success?

That is where we go next.

CHAPTER 9

When to Engage a Fractional Executive

The companies engaging Fractional Executives generally fall into the small- and medium-sized category, typically with less than $100M in revenue and fewer than 100 employees. Roles in functions like marketing, sales, finance, and operations are well-suited to Fractional Leadership. Others, such as manufacturing plant management, are not, as those roles require a constant on-site presence. Fractional CFOs, by contrast, are among the oldest and most established fractional roles, since financial strategy does not require daily involvement once proper systems are in place.

About Inflection Points and Unlimited Scenarios

When companies decide to engage a Fractional Executive, it rarely happens during calm, steady periods of business. It is almost always triggered by specific challenges, disruptions, or periods of complexity. These moments force a founder, owner, or CEO to seek out help.

Their first instinct is usually not to hire a Fractional Executive. Instead, they look for solutions or inflection points, periods where a shift in market conditions, technology, or customer behavior changes the trajectory of growth. They ask their network, speak with their leadership team and Board members, or recall something they've read.

It's important to recognize that there are essentially unlimited scenarios in which fractional help is appropriate. Any meaningful business problem that requires specialized expertise and additional bandwidth can justify the use of a Fractional Executive. Fractionals offer two things simultaneously:

1. Know-how: the expertise to understand and solve the problem, and

2. Manpower: the hours required to implement the solution.

Most small businesses lack one or both. A CEO may know what needs to be fixed but lacks the time; or they have the resource but lack the experience. Fractional Executives solve both sides of that equation. And crucially, they can be right-sized and right-skilled to the specific need. Once the problem is resolved, the company can end the engagement with no ongoing obligation.

Companies engage Fractionals for two types of scenarios:

1. They have a problem and don't know the solution, so they need an executive to diagnose and solve it.
2. They have a problem and know the solution, but they lack the resources or expertise to execute it.

In both cases, Fractional Leaders bring focused attention and skill. One example was a client with 20 sales reps, each using a different process. They knew the solution was a formal playbook reflecting best practices, but they lacked the ability to design one. The Fractional Executive consolidated 20 versions into one best-practice model and turned it into a structured training manual. That required both expertise and time.

This is also where the most common inflection points show up:

- Plateauing growth: a business has momentum, but something in the function is now limiting scale.

- Entering new markets: a new geography, vertical, channel, or product line introduces complexity and demands specialized expertise.
- Preparing for fundraising or exit: the business needs discipline, credibility, systems, reporting, and leadership maturity.
- Professionalizing a founder-led function: the founder has carried the function as long as possible, and now the "multi-hat model" becomes the bottleneck.

For small- and medium-sized businesses navigating today's uncertain economic environment, one of the most consequential inflection points is the rise of AI. From marketing automation to sales enablement and even talent acquisition, AI is rapidly reshaping how companies operate. For founders, owners, and CEOs, this shift presents both opportunity and confusion.

AI promises efficiency. It accelerates tasks that once consumed time and headcount: writing content, analyzing data, scoring leads, drafting job descriptions, or automating processes. For resource-constrained businesses, that promise is compelling. When margins are tight and teams are lean, automation feels like relief.

But AI also introduces a new form of risk: false confidence.

Many leaders assume that because AI can generate answers, it can also generate judgment. In practice, AI excels at pattern recognition and execution, but it does not understand context, trade-offs, or timing. It cannot assess whether a sales motion is premature, whether a market is ready, or whether a company has the operational maturity to support growth. Those decisions still require experience.

This is where Fractional Executives increasingly enter the picture.

Rather than replacing leadership, AI often exposes its absence. Founders, owners, and CEOs quickly discover that while tools can execute faster, they still need someone to decide what to execute, when, and why. Automation without strategy amplifies mistakes just as easily as it amplifies success.

Fractional Executives sit at the intersection of this inflection point. They bring human judgment to an increasingly automated environment. A Fractional Sales Leader may leverage AI-driven forecasting or CRM automation, but they also understand sales cycles, buyer behavior, and organizational readiness. A Fractional Marketing Leader may deploy AI-generated content, but they still define positioning, audience, and channel strategy. AI accelerates execution; Fractional Leadership ensures direction.

This inflection point is not about choosing between AI and people. It is about recognizing that as tools become more powerful, leadership decisions become more consequential. The cost of doing the wrong thing faster is often higher than the cost of doing the right thing deliberately.

For many founders, owners, and CEOs, engaging a Fractional Executive at this moment allows them to harness AI responsibly. The executive helps determine which tools matter, how they fit the business model, and where human oversight is non-negotiable. Instead of chasing every new platform or shortcut, the company gains clarity, sequencing, and restraint.

In that sense, AI does not eliminate the need for Fractional Leadership; it often accelerates it. The businesses that navigate this inflection point successfully are not those with the most tools, but those with the clearest judgment guiding their use.

Timing: Hiring Too Late vs. Too Early

Timing is one of the most underestimated variables in fractional success. Hiring too early and hiring too late both carry real consequences, and in practice, many failed engagements trace back to timing errors rather than capability gaps.

Hiring too early usually stems from optimism. A founder recognizes a problem and assumes that bringing in an executive, fractional or full-time, will immediately produce results. Revenue will accelerate. Systems will fall into place. Order will replace chaos. But executive leadership does not compress time. Sales cycles remain sales cycles. Markets still need to be educated. Teams still need to be built, trained, and aligned.

When companies hire too early, they often lack the foundational elements required for an executive to succeed. There may be an insufficient financial runway to sustain the engagement long enough for impact to materialize. Product-market fit may still be evolving. Data may be incomplete or unreliable. In these situations, even a highly capable executive ends up managing uncertainty rather than driving progress. The work becomes reactive rather than strategic, and the engagement ends prematurely, not because the Executive failed, but because the business was not yet ready to absorb the leadership leverage.

Hiring too late creates a different set of risks.

In these cases, companies delay bringing in help until the situation becomes urgent. Growth has plateaued. Customers are churning. Forecasts are being missed. Teams are burned out. The founder is firefighting across multiple functions with no time to think strategically. By the time an Executive is engaged, expectations are compressed, and pressure is high. The mandate quietly becomes: "Fix this now."

Late hiring often leads to unrealistic timelines and misplaced accountability. Structural problems that developed over the years are expected to be resolved in weeks. The Executive is brought in to stabilize, rebuild, and accelerate simultaneously. While Fractional Leaders are often brought in precisely because they can operate under pressure, even they cannot reverse compounded issues overnight. When urgency replaces realism, trust erodes quickly.

There are also external timing factors that founders, owners, and CEOs frequently overlook. For example, large retailers like Walmart evaluate new vendors only during designated periods each year. Some companies make the bulk of their sales in the months leading up to the holidays. Others have annual trade shows where new products must be ready. Fractional Leadership needs to align with those cycles just as full-time hiring does. Hiring an Executive outside of those cycles will delay impact regardless of effort. A Fractional Leader may do everything right yet still appear ineffective simply because the market timing is misaligned.

The healthiest engagements occur in the middle ground.

The company has enough runway to support the work. The problem is clear, even if the solution is not. Leadership recognizes that results require sequencing, not miracles. The Executive is engaged early enough to prevent damage but late enough to enable the business to actually execute on recommendations.

Outside of those external considerations, the rule of thumb is simple: the sooner, the better. Once you recognize a problem, delaying the solution only prolongs the damage.

Fractional Executives do their best when they are given room to diagnose, design, and deliver rather than being asked to rescue a situation that timing already made fragile.

Case Example:
When Timing Undermines the Engagement

An early-stage founder engaged a Fractional Sales Leader to accelerate revenue growth. The product showed promise, the market appeared receptive, and the founder believed that bringing in experienced sales leadership would immediately unlock growth.

What the founder underestimated was time.

The sales cycle in this market was long, measured in months, not weeks. While the Fractional Executive did exactly what they were hired to do, diagnosing the sales motion, refining positioning, building pipeline discipline, and laying the groundwork for scale, the company's financial runway was simply too short. After only a few months, cash constraints forced the engagement to end.

From the outside, it looked like a failure of the fractional model. It wasn't.

The executive delivered appropriately for the scope and stage of the business. The breakdown occurred in planning. Expectations for speed did not align with market realities, and the company engaged senior leadership without sufficient runway to allow results to materialize.

The lesson is straightforward: Fractional Leadership can accelerate outcomes, but it cannot change realities. Sales cycles, market adoption, and operational change still take time. Engaging a Fractional Executive too late or without adequate financial and strategic planning can undermine even a well-matched, well-executed engagement.

ROI Analysis: Fractional vs. Full-Time (and the Cost of Doing Nothing)

When founders, owners, and CEOs evaluate whether to hire a Fractional Executive or a full-time leader, the conversation often starts in the wrong place: hourly rates versus salary. Fractional rates can look high when viewed in isolation. Full-time salaries, by contrast, feel predictable and familiar. But ROI is not about which option looks cheaper on paper. It is about which option produces results faster, with less risk, and with better alignment to the company's actual stage and needs.

To evaluate ROI correctly, three factors must be considered together:

1. The fully loaded cost of full-time leadership
2. The speed and impact of fractional deployment
3. The cost of delayed or incorrect decisions

Only when all three are examined does the economic logic of Fractional Leadership become clear.

A full-time executive's salary is only the starting point. Once benefits, payroll taxes, bonuses, equity, recruiting fees, onboarding time, training, and opportunity costs are included, the total annual cost is often up to 2x higher than base compensation alone.

For example, a VP of Sales with a base salary of $180,000 may represent:

- $180,000 base salary
- $30,000–$50,000 in bonuses or incentives
- $25,000–$40,000 in benefits and payroll burden
- $30,000–$50,000 in recruiting and onboarding costs

The real first-year cost can easily exceed $260,000–$300,000, before any measurable impact is delivered.

More importantly, most SMBs do not yet need—or cannot yet fully utilize—40+ hours per week of executive leadership in a single function. What they need is targeted expertise applied at the right moments: diagnosing the bottleneck, designing systems, coaching leaders, and building a structure that will outlast the engagement.

Fractional Leadership enables companies to buy leadership capacity in precise increments rather than all at once.

Many fractional engagements fall within the $8,000–$12,000 per month range. Over six months, that represents an investment of $48,000–$72,000.

That is still meaningful money for an SMB—but it is materially different from committing to a quarter-million-dollar hire before the company is structurally ready to absorb it.

More importantly, the goal of fractional work is not to replace full-time leadership indefinitely. It is to:

- Build systems
- Professionalize functions
- Reduce founder dependency
- Prepare the organization for the next stage of growth

In many cases, the Fractional Executive's role is to create the conditions under which a future full-time hire can actually succeed.

From a ROI standpoint, this sequencing matters. Hiring too early leads to wasted spend. Hiring too late leads to compounded operational damage. Fractional Leadership sits in the middle, allowing companies to invest in progress without overcommitting capital or organizational bandwidth.

ROI is not only about cost. It is about how quickly problems are identified and corrected.

Fractional Executives are typically hired because they have already solved similar problems multiple times. They recognize patterns quickly. They know where to look first. They do not require months to understand what is broken, what is missing, or what must change.

This density of experiences compresses and nearly eliminates learning curves.

A full-time executive may spend months diagnosing before implementing. A Fractional Leader is often implementing while diagnosing, because the situations are familiar. That speed reduces the duration of underperformance and shortens the time to measurable improvement.

When revenue is plateauing, margins are shrinking, or teams are misaligned, every week of delay has a real financial cost. Fractional Leadership often delivers ROI by reducing the time a company operates inefficiently.

The Cost of Doing Nothing

The most overlooked part of an ROI analysis for a Fractional Executive is not the cost of hiring—it is the cost of waiting.

When companies delay leadership investment because they cannot afford a full-time hire, the underlying problems continue to compound:

- Inefficient processes become entrenched
- Poor hiring decisions multiply
- Founder burnout increases
- Revenue opportunities are missed

- Customer experience deteriorates
- Technical debt and operational shortcuts accumulate

These costs rarely appear as a single line item, yet they are often far more expensive than the leadership investment required to prevent them.

Spending $60,000 over six months to correct sales execution, professionalize operations, or stabilize cash flow can easily prevent losses several times that amount over the following year. In this sense, Fractional Leadership is not just a growth investment; it is often a risk mitigation strategy.

Choosing not to act is still a decision—and it frequently turns out to be the most expensive one.

Another dimension of ROI is strategic flexibility. Full-time hires are difficult to reverse. Terminations are disruptive, costly, and culturally damaging. Fractional engagements, by contrast, can be scaled, reshaped, or concluded with far less organizational friction.

This flexibility has economic value. It allows companies to:

- Redirect resources as strategy evolves
- Add specialized expertise temporarily
- Support transformation initiatives without permanent headcount
- Reduce downside risk if assumptions prove incorrect

From a ROI standpoint, this optionality matters. It allows leadership teams to test and adapt without betting the company on a single long-term hiring decision.

While revenue growth and cost savings are easy to measure, some of the most powerful returns from Fractional Leadership are structural and cultural:

- Clearer decision-making
- Stronger management accountability
- Better data and forecasting
- Reduced founder dependency
- Higher-quality hiring standards
- Increased investor confidence

These benefits compound over time. They increase the effectiveness of every subsequent hire and initiative.

In many cases, the Fractional Executive's greatest ROI is not what they personally deliver, but what they enable the organization to do better after they leave.

When evaluating fractional versus full-time leadership, founders, owners, and CEOs should ask five practical questions:

1. What specific outcomes must be achieved in the next 6–12 months?
2. How much executive capacity is truly required to achieve them?
3. What is the financial impact of achieving—or not achieving—those outcomes?
4. How quickly must change occur to protect growth or stability?
5. What is the cost of being wrong in this decision?

When framed this way, the question often shifts from "Which option is cheaper?" to "Which option reduces risk and accelerates results?"

In many SMB scenarios, the answer is fractional.

Ultimately, ROI in leadership is not about permanence. It is about precision. Precision in matching expertise to problems, matching time commitment to workload, and matching investment to growth stage.

Fractional Leadership works because it allows companies to invest with precision instead of committing capital and organizational structure in large, inflexible steps.

And in growth environments where uncertainty is constant and resources are finite, precision is often the most valuable asset of all.

The Window of Opportunity

"A Window of Opportunity is a period of time during which some action can be taken that will achieve a desired outcome. Once this period is over, or the window is closed, the specified outcome is no longer possible."

The ideal timing, or the Window of Opportunity, for placing a Fractional Executive varies based on factors such as the organization's needs, the specific C-suite function, team size, revenue growth, and organizational maturity. Understanding this window is critical for the business to optimize the value of a Fractional Executive. And equally essential for the Executive themselves to understand and target their Ideal Client Profile.

Revenue growth is one catalyst. A business generating $1M in revenue may not yet require a full-time CFO, but when revenues grow tenfold, financial oversight becomes more complex. In this case, a Fractional CFO can step in to build scalable financial systems, support fundraising efforts, or guide mergers and acquisitions.

Team size is another. A company experiencing growth may suddenly find itself with a sales team of 5 or more individuals, yet without a formal sales leader. A Fractional CRO or Head of Sales is ideal in this scenario, offering strategic oversight to scale processes, implement metrics, and coach the team without the delay of recruiting a full-time leader.

And maturity matters. Early-stage companies often rely on founders to wear multiple hats, but this model becomes unsustainable as the business matures. The introduction of a Fractional Executive at this juncture allows founders to focus on their core strengths while delegating specialized leadership functions.

Deploy a Fractional Executive when:

- You're scaling rapidly: teams without a leader, revenue doubling, or departments misaligned.
- A specific high-leverage project is underway: M&A, fund raising, restructuring, tech integration, or market pivot.
- Full-time hires are premature or unaffordable, yet executive-level guidance is essential.

This is the Window of Opportunity; when you need momentum and structure at the same time, and you cannot afford to slow down long enough to "wait until you're ready" for a full-time hire. Fractional lets you move fast, with executive support, without over-hiring.

CHAPTER 10

How to Integrate a Fractional Leader

Fractional Executives are a powerful tool in the modern leader's toolkit, especially for start-ups, scale-ups, SMBs, and any company on a fast-growth or transition path. They bring C-suite horsepower at a fraction of the cost, accelerate transformation, and offer catalytic leadership on demand.

Many fractional frameworks emphasize a robust vetting process to minimize misalignment, but even the best matching system cannot compensate for unclear expectations or a lack of executive support. Their success hinges on alignment: clarity in purpose, integration into the leadership team, and a vision that values change. With that context, the Fractional Executive transforms from a temporary placeholder into a strategic accelerant and sometimes the beginning of a lasting executive partnership.

The rise of Fractional Executives, seasoned C-suite leaders working part-time across multiple organizations, offers a compelling strategic alternative for companies navigating growth, transition, or strategic shifts. The model brings agility and expertise. It also comes with limits. Fractional is powerful, but it isn't universal.

When Is a Fractional Executive the Right Fit?

A true Fractional Executive role is generally not a fit for a Fortune 1,000 company, maybe even a Fortune 5,000 company. Those companies require too much knowledge of internal processes and procedures, and also operate with too much internal focus, conditions that a Fractional

Executive is generally not equipped to handle. Their teams of direct and indirect reports for an executive function are also too large to be managed part-time.

Fractional Executives tend to create the most leverage where the organization is small enough for a senior leader to see the whole system, but complex enough that the founder cannot carry it alone.

Fractional Leaders are growth catalysts, not maintenance managers. They seek to drive transformation, uplift stagnant performance, and challenge the status quo. If the organization aims to preserve current operations, a part-time manager might suffice, but truly impactful Fractional Executives demand a mandate to lead change.

This is a subtle but critical distinction. Fractional works best when the founder, owner, or CEO is willing to let the executive lead rather than simply advise.

A Fractional Executive must be fully aligned with the CEO's strategic vision. They thrive when treated as equals in the leadership team. Without transparency, where their purpose, selection rationale, and performance criteria are clearly communicated, the engagement falters. Openness within the executive team is essential. A Fractional Leader must feel welcome and empowered across departments to gain traction.

This is not about titles or optics. It is about whether the organization will accept leadership from 'someone who is not "full-time." If the answer is no, the model will fail, even if the executive is exceptional.

While their cash rate may exceed a traditional salary basis, Fractional Executives offer immense value:

- No benefits, equity, bonuses, or recruitment costs.
- You pay only for the time and expertise you need.

This model is financially sound, especially when foundational gaps can inhibit growth. Fractional is not simply a cheaper version of full-time. It is a different way to buy leadership: **right-sized, right-skilled**, and time-bound.

Fractional Leaders often carry decades of domain experience and bring a breadth of cross-industry insight. They spotlight process inefficiencies, questionable arrangements, and strategic blind spots. Their external perspective helps them speak candidly, less influenced by internal politics, more focused on truth and outcomes.

It is worthwhile mentioning that engaging a Fractional Executive does come with some trade-offs:

- Divided attention: They balance multiple clients, meaning they're not available 24/7. Managing expectations mitigates this risk.
- Limited cultural immersion: Part-time status may inhibit full integration. Success requires openness and alignment from the internal team.
- Matching risk: A wrong pairing, skills-wise or culture-wise, can derail the engagement. A deliberate selection process and a clear mandate are musts.

With rising employment costs, regulatory pressure, and skill shortages, agility matters. Fractional Executives give companies access to high-level capability without the long ramp-up or long-term commitment that often delays action.

A Guide to Identifying a Great Fractional Sales Leader

Many companies are turning to Fractional Sales Leaders to drive growth without the commitment of a full-time executive. These seasoned professionals offer strategic sales expertise on a part-time basis, providing flexibility and cost-effectiveness. For founders, owners, and CEOs considering this approach, identifying the right Fractional Sales Leader is crucial.

The following attributes increase the odds of a high-impact engagement.

Extensive Sales Leadership Experience: A top-tier Fractional Sales Leader brings a wealth of experience from diverse industries and company sizes. This background enables them to adapt strategies to your company's unique challenges and opportunities. Their track record should include driving revenue growth, building high-performing teams, and entering new markets.

Strategic Vision and Execution: Beyond day-to-day management, an effective Fractional Sales Leader possesses the ability to develop and implement long-term sales strategies aligned with your company's objectives. They should be adept at identifying target markets, refining value propositions, and creating scalable sales processes.

Data-Driven Decision Making: In the modern sales landscape, leveraging data is essential. Seek a leader who utilizes analytics to assess performance, forecast trends, and inform strategic decisions. Their proficiency with CRM systems and sales analytics tools will be instrumental in optimizing your sales operations.

Adaptability and Flexibility: The fractional nature of the role demands a leader who can quickly acclimate to your company's culture and industry dynamics. They should be able to adjust strategies in response to market shifts and internal changes, ensuring resilience and agility in your sales approach.

Strong Communication and Interpersonal Skills: Effective communication is vital for aligning sales teams and articulating strategies to stakeholders. A Fractional Sales Leader must excel in conveying ideas clearly, listening actively, and fostering collaboration across departments. Their ability to build trust and rapport will facilitate the smoother implementation of sales initiatives.

Proven Ability to Develop and Mentor Teams: Building a high-performing sales team is a hallmark of exceptional leadership. Look for a Fractional Sales Leader who prioritizes talent development, offering coaching and mentorship to enhance individual and collective performance. Their focus on nurturing skills and fostering a positive culture will have lasting benefits.

Objective Perspective: As an external member of your organization, a Fractional Sales Leader provides an unbiased assessment of your sales operations. This objectivity allows them to identify inefficiencies and recommend improvements without being influenced by internal politics.

Cost-Effectiveness: One of the primary advantages of hiring a Fractional Sales Leader is access to high-level expertise without the financial commitment of a full-time executive. Ensure that the leader's compensation aligns with your budget while delivering the desired impact.

Clear Track Record of Results: Request case studies or references that demonstrate the leader's ability to deliver tangible outcomes, such as increased revenue, improved sales processes, or successful market expansion. This evidence provides confidence in their capacity to contribute meaningfully.

Cultural Fit: While the engagement may be part-time, the Fractional Sales Leader will play a significant role in your organization. Assess whether their leadership style and values align with your company's culture to promote seamless integration and collaboration.

Selecting the right Fractional Sales Leader requires careful evaluation of experience, strategic capability, adaptability, and alignment with your company's needs and culture. When those elements align, Fractional Sales Leadership becomes a force multiplier, bringing senior horsepower into the business at exactly the right scale.

However, interviewing Fractional Executives for Sales Roles may require a different approach to traditional hiring practices and includes distinct considerations, such as their specific skills, immediate effectiveness, and cultural fit within your organization.

Interview Checklist

"Why did you end up in Sales?" is my favorite interview question, and the answers vary widely. These responses often reflect the candidate's motivation for pursuing a career in sales, such as family influence, financial needs, or a genuine passion for the field. Sales roles are multifaceted and demand attributes such as ambition, a growth mindset, and the ability to connect with people.

Sales job interviews typically focus on questions that assess knowledge, experience, and future goals. Common examples include asking about the candidate's understanding of the company, their career overview, and their strategies for generating and closing opportunities. These open-ended questions help assess past experiences, current interests, and future aspirations.

When interviewing Fractional Executive candidates for any functional capacity, several factors set the process apart from speaking with traditional, full-time sales candidates:

1. Specific Task Focus: Fractional Executives are hired for a particular task or period, making it crucial to evaluate their skills for achieving short-term goals efficiently.

2. Immediate Effectiveness: These candidates are expected to deliver results without a steep learning curve, emphasizing relevant past experiences and skills.

3. Part-Time Contractors: Unlike full-time employees, Fractional Executives typically are lower risk hires and do not require extensive rounds of interviews. They bring extensive experience and a focus on strategic leadership.

4. Multiple Engagements: Fractional Executives often balance multiple engagements simultaneously, requiring commitment from the hiring company. Delayed decisions will lead them to pursue other opportunities.

The Thing About Cultural Fit

Cultural fit is critical in any hiring decision because it influences harmony between employees and the work environment. A study found that 82% of hiring managers consider cultural fit important[22]. Candidates must align with a company's values, beliefs, and behaviors to ensure a successful and satisfying work experience.

For Fractional Executives, though, functional job fit takes precedence given the task-specific nature of their roles. While cultural fit is important, the immediate need for skills and results makes it the primary consideration during the interview process.

Interviewing Fractional Executive candidates requires a tailored approach focused on immediate skills, task-specific effectiveness, and alignment with organizational goals. While cultural fit remains important, it should complement job fit within the unique context of

---

[22] https://www.amazon.com/Pedigree-How-Elite-Students-Jobs/dp/0691169276

fractional work. By accounting for these differences, founders, owners, and CEOs can make better decisions and avoid costly mismatches.

Integration:
How Fractional Leaders Function Inside the Business

Leaders often ask how to integrate a Fractional Executive into their organization. The answer is simple: exactly the same way as a full-time leader. Introduce them to the team. Bring them into executive meetings. Give them a company email. Add them to the website. Encourage them to identify publicly with the role on LinkedIn. This conveys commitment and helps them function as a genuine member of the leadership team.

"This is our CFO," not "This is our fractional finance guy."

Clear expectations must be established upfront. This includes defining outcomes, setting realistic targets, and capturing these expectations in the contract. Executives must ensure that the founder's, owner's, and CEO's expectations align with reality before they begin. A mismatch on day one is a recipe for disappointment.

A 30/60/90-day plan is always helpful. Early wins build credibility and momentum. You don't start with the biggest, most complex initiative; you begin with achievable milestones that demonstrate value.

To establish cultural integration with the Fractional Executive, consider the following actions when onboarding:

1. **Warm Welcome**: Provide Fractional Executives with the same welcome, onboarding, and orientation as full-time employees to make a positive impression from the start.
2. **Team Integration**: Introduce them to the team, highlighting their past achievements and the role's significance.

3. **Recognition**: Recognize and acknowledge their contributions to foster motivation and buy-in.

4. **Goal Alignment**: Explain how their work aligns with broader organizational goals to give purpose.

5. **Feedback Loop**: Offer regular performance appraisals and feedback so they feel invested and can contribute efficiently.

6. **Inclusion in Social Gatherings**: Encourage participation to build belonging within the team.

Fractional Executives must help and guide founders, owners, and CEOs through this process. Most have never worked with a Fractional before, whereas the Fractional Executive has extensive experience integrating into new organizations, leading teams, and solving similar problems.

A Fractional shouldn't be a passive yes-sayer. Their value comes from speaking up, challenging assumptions, and applying their expertise, much like a trusted advisor.

Guardrails are important as well. Founders, owners, and CEOs may be tempted to use a Fractional as extra hands for unrelated tasks. A Fractional Leader must maintain the boundaries of their scope and guide the CEO back to the agreed-upon priorities.

Performance measurement comes through KPIs and milestones. These should be specific to the problem the Fractional is hired to solve. For example:

- "First draft of the playbook in eight weeks."
- "Interview all 20 reps by week four."
- "Ten prospect outreaches by week four, five meetings by week eight, two closed deals by week twelve."

These KPIs can be embedded into any system the company already uses, such as the Entrepreneurial Operating System (EOS), CRM dashboards, Enterprise Resource Planning (ERP) data, shared documents; or these systems need to be created if none exist. The executive adapts to the company's tools or introduces new ones where necessary.

Fractional Leadership is a proven solution across many functional areas, and when integrated correctly, with clear goals, communication, boundaries, and performance metrics, it creates meaningful impact without the long-term cost or commitment of full-time hiring.

As a founder, owner, or CEO, making an informed decision is essential; it's important to consider the right factors and all available data.

Onboarding Fractional Executives

The success of a fractional engagement is often decided before any meaningful work begins. Unlike full-time executives, Fractional Leaders are brought in to create impact quickly. That speed advantage disappears if onboarding is casual, fragmented, or treated as an afterthought. Fractional Executives do not require less structure because they are part-time; they require *more* clarity because the margin for error is smaller.

Effective onboarding rests on five foundations: communication, process, team alignment, outcomes, and culture. When any one of these is neglected, momentum slows. When all five are handled deliberately, Fractional Leaders integrate faster and deliver value sooner.

Clear, consistent communication is the backbone of a successful fractional engagement. From day one, the CEO must set and maintain a review cadence. Regular check-ins are not optional, especially during the onboarding period. Missed meetings, long gaps in feedback, or vague updates send an unintended signal that the work of the Fractional is secondary. It isn't.

The Fractional Executive's role must also be communicated clearly to the leadership team and the wider organization. Ambiguity invites resistance. When people don't understand why the Fractional Leader is there, or what authority they hold, progress stalls quietly through hesitation, side conversations, or passive noncompliance.

Urgency matters as well. A Fractional Leader's scope of work should be treated as a priority initiative, not something that fits in "when there's time." Clear communication around goals, timelines, and expectations creates focus and signals that leadership is aligned behind the engagement.

Fractional Executives cannot create impact without access. They must have immediate access to the tools, systems, data, and people required for their role. Delays in system access, financial data, or stakeholder availability can stall progress for weeks and waste valuable contract time.

One of the fastest ways to derail a fractional engagement is to leave the executive waiting. Waiting on logins. Waiting on introductions. Waiting on decisions. If access to systems or people will be blocked, the start date should be delayed until the organization is truly ready to onboard.

Just as importantly, companies should not assume a Fractional Executive can self-onboard into internal processes. Even the most experienced leader needs a proper kickoff. A structured onboarding session that explains how decisions are made, how work flows, and where information lives creates a clear pathway into the organization.

Aligning on a visible quick win in the first 30 to 45 days is equally critical. Early momentum builds credibility, reinforces confidence, and demonstrates value to the broader team.

Before a Fractional Executive is introduced to the team, key stakeholders must already be aligned. If senior leaders or influential team members are not on board with the role, resistance and hidden politics will quietly undermine progress.

Transparency is essential. Fractional Leaders should clearly understand the organizational chart, reporting lines, and team dynamics. Challenges within the team, such as political tensions, prior failures, and legacy relationships, should not be hidden in an effort to "keep things positive." Withholding context forces the Fractional Executive to discover obstacles the hard way, slowing progress and eroding trust.

Even when teams are busy, leadership must not disappear during onboarding. Ghosting a Fractional Executive, missing meetings, delaying responses, or deprioritizing communication leaves them operating in a silo.

A Fractional Executive should never be judged against undefined or shifting expectations. From the start, the scope of work must be clearly documented, including deliverables, performance metrics, and strategic context. Without this clarity, even strong performers can appear ineffective.

Timelines matter as much as goals. Unrealistic expectations about the pace of change create pressure to rush work that requires sequencing and patience. The goal is progress, not theater.

Trust must be established immediately. Important context, data, and strategic considerations should not be withheld. Best practice is to co-sign an NDA early and operate with full transparency from day one. As priorities shift, as they inevitably will, milestones should be revisited and adjusted openly. This protects both the executive and the organization.

Fractional Executives must be valued the same as a full-time executive in the role. The classification is irrelevant; accountability is not. Fractional Leaders should be trusted to steer within their scope and held fully responsible for outcomes.

Closed mindsets undermine the model. Micromanagement, second-guessing, or assumptions about "all Fractional Leaders" create strive before results have a chance to materialize. Each Fractional Executive brings a unique set of strengths, patterns, and working styles. Success depends on thorough vetting, clear mutual expectations, and a willingness to trust the leader.

Fractional Leadership is a different working model. Like any new model, it requires openness, discipline, and intentionality. When organizations approach onboarding thoughtfully, communicating clearly, aligning teams, defining outcomes, and reinforcing respect, they create the conditions for Fractional Executives to do what they were hired to do: deliver meaningful impact quickly and responsibly.

Case Example:
When Integration Makes the Difference

A founder-led Business-to-Business (B2B) services company with roughly 60 employees had reached a familiar breaking point. Revenue growth had slowed, the sales team was frustrated, and forecasting had become unreliable. The founder knew the business needed senior sales leadership but could not justify the cost or risk of a full-time hire. Instead, they engaged a Fractional Chief Revenue Officer with deep experience scaling similar organizations.

On paper, the match was strong. The executive had led multiple teams through comparable growth stages and came highly recommended.

What made the engagement successful, however, was not the resume. It was how the company integrated the Fractional Leader from day one.

Before the executive's start date, the CEO took several deliberate steps. The leadership team was briefed in advance, not just on who was coming in, but why. The message was clear: this was not a consultant offering advice from the sidelines. This was the company's CRO, responsible for leading revenue strategy and execution.

On day one, the fractional CRO had full access to CRM, dashboards, historical performance data, and direct introductions to sales managers and key stakeholders. There were no delays waiting on permissions or explanations. A kickoff session clarified how decisions were made, how priorities were set, and where the executive had authority to act.

Equally important, expectations were explicit. The scope of work was documented in advance, with clear outcomes rather than vague goals. The first 30–60–90 days focused on achievable milestones: interviewing the entire sales team, consolidating inconsistent processes into a single playbook, and establishing a weekly operating rhythm. These early wins built credibility quickly.

The CEO also protected time. Weekly meetings were never skipped. Feedback flowed in both directions. When assumptions were challenged, the CEO listened. When priorities shifted, they were discussed openly and reset together. Trust was built early, and with it, momentum.

As pressure mounted elsewhere in the business, the CEO resisted the temptation to pull the fractional CRO into unrelated operational work. When requests drifted outside scope, the executive redirected the conversation back to agreed priorities without conflict because those boundaries had already been established.

Performance was measured by outcomes rather than hours. No one tracked the time spent. Instead, leadership tracked progress: clearer pipeline visibility, consistent sales methodology, improved conversion rates, and a noticeable shift in team confidence. Within six months, revenue growth resumed, forecasting stabilized, and the sales organization operated with a level of discipline it had never had before.

The engagement lasted longer than initially planned. Eventually, the company chose to convert the role into a permanent position but by then, the risk had already been mitigated. The fractional model had allowed the company to buy leadership at the right scale, prove value before committing long-term, and integrate change without disruption.

CHAPTER 11

The Matchmaking Process

Artificial intelligence has reshaped how founders, owners, and CEOs think about hiring. For time-pressed leaders, the appeal is obvious: generate a job description in minutes, identify candidates on your own, filter resumes automatically, and even score applicants without involving a recruiting partner. On the surface, it feels faster, cheaper, and more scalable.

But leadership hiring, especially for Fractional Sales roles, doesn't behave like other hiring problems.

We've seen this pattern before. When online travel platforms emerged, many assumed travel agents would disappear entirely. For simple trips, they largely did. But for complex, high-stakes, highly specific, or luxury travel, experienced advisors remain indispensable. The same principle applies to executive placement. AI can support the process, but it cannot replace the depth of judgment, context, and pattern recognition required to place a Fractional Leader who can drive revenue, align with a founder's vision, and operate effectively at a specific growth stage.

Small- and medium-sized businesses are particularly vulnerable to the illusion of Do It Yourself (DIY) hiring. Lean teams and constrained budgets make automation feel like a smart shortcut. A few LinkedIn posts, a set of AI-generated interview questions, and recruiting starts to look like just another workflow to optimize. In reality, this oversimplification often masks the real risk.

The cost of a misaligned sales leader is not theoretical. It shows up as stalled momentum, lost customer credibility, internal churn, and delayed growth. AI promises efficiency, but in leadership hiring, the wrong hire is the most expensive inefficiency a business can absorb.

This chapter covers what actually happens **behind the scenes in a high-quality match** and why fit is something you build deliberately, not something you stumble upon by comparing profiles.

To be clear, this is not an argument against AI. At Vendux, technology plays an important role in how we operate, from market mapping to executive onboarding. But AI works best as an amplifier of human judgment, not a replacement for it. The strongest outcomes occur when technology enhances insight, rather than attempting to shortcut it.

For companies navigating growth, transition, or uncertainty, the goal isn't to hire faster at any cost. It's to place the right leader in the right role at the right moment. For Fractional Executives, that requires judgment shaped by experience, context, and pattern recognition, capabilities that still live firmly on the human side of the equation.

Once it's clear that leadership matching cannot be automated or rushed without consequence, the next question becomes practical: where do the right Fractional Leaders actually come from?

High-quality matches are not the result of posting a role and waiting. They are built through deliberate sourcing across multiple channels, each with its own strengths, limitations, and risks. Understanding how these channels work and when each is appropriate matters just as much as evaluating the executive once they're identified.

In Fractional Leadership, sourcing is not about volume. It's about access. The goal is not to attract the largest possible pool of candidates, but to attract a small number of executives who are already qualified, available, and suited to the company's specific stage and challenge.

That process begins with where and how leaders are found.

Sourcing Channels

When CEOs imagine "recruiting," they often think of one channel: posting a role and waiting. That model is slow even for full-time hiring. For Fractional hiring, where timing matters and the expectation is immediate effectiveness, it's often the wrong model entirely.

In Fractional Leadership placement, sourcing is multi-channel by design. The highest-quality matches typically emerge from a combination of:

1) Direct Outreach

Direct outreach is still one of the most powerful sourcing engines, especially when it's relationship-driven and role-specific. The best executives are not always actively looking. Many are already fully engaged. Others are only selectively available. And most don't respond to generic "opportunities."

Direct outreach works when it's grounded in a clear scenario: Here is the company's stage, here is the problem, and here is the mandate. That kind of precision attracts the right leaders and filters out everyone else.

2) Platforms and Networks

There are platforms, networks, and ecosystems that matter in this space and that aggregate serious operators. These systems can create speed and reach, but they only work when there is a meaningful layer of intelligence on top.

A platform can help find candidates. It cannot, on its own, identify which candidate will succeed within *your* business, given *your* constraints and under *your* CEO.

That is why it is important to separate the two ideas that people confuse:

- **Sourcing** is finding the pool.
- **Matching** is narrowing to the few who are actually right.

3) Referrals

Referrals can be high-signal, but they are not automatically high-fit.

Investors and peers often refer people they trust personally. That's valuable. But trust is not the same as alignment. The referred executive may be excellent, just not excellent for *this* stage, *this* sales motion, or *this* operating environment.

Referrals should be treated as a sourcing channel, not a shortcut to proper matching. The match still needs to be built.

Evaluating Fit

Unlike entry-level or transactional roles, Fractional Leadership is a nuanced match of experience, temperament, industry insight, and strategic acumen. An algorithm might identify a candidate with 20 years in B2B SaaS, but only a human conversation will reveal whether they can coach a struggling sales team, align with a founder's vision, or scale a $5M business to $20M.

At Vendux, we use a proprietary system called PerfectMatch™ that goes far beyond resumes and keyword matching. We evaluate context: what does the business actually need at this moment? Do they require transformation or stabilization? Are they entering a new market, or optimizing an existing one? And above everything, what past experiences will actually make an executive successful?

These subtleties are difficult, if not impossible, to codify into an AI model without introducing risk. Our pre-vetted roster of currently over

1,400 executives isn't just a database but a living network of leaders we know very well, trust, and can confidently recommend.

But here's the real point: even a deep roster is useless if you don't know what "fit" means.

Fit in fractional work is usually a combination of three things:

1) Technical Expertise

When people talk about matching executives with companies, whether for full-time roles or fractional engagements, they often assume it's as simple as comparing resumes or LinkedIn profiles. But a perfect match requires far more than scanning resumes.

Most public profiles lack the depth and detail needed to make a true assessment. Key information, such as revenue responsibility, profitability impact, team size, sales KPIs, and customer volume, is rarely included because the data is often confidential or considered proprietary. And yet, these are exactly the data points that matter.

Even when executives describe their experience, the language is vague. Someone might claim they've "done enterprise sales," but that can mean many different things. For one executive, an enterprise deal might be $50,000. For another, it might be $10M. Those are entirely different realities requiring different skill sets. Without probing deeper, it's impossible to know whether an executive is suited to a company's specific scenario.

Brand names can also be misleading. Many people market themselves as "ex-Google" or "ex-Oracle," but that may represent a seven-month stint in a mid-level role, too brief or insignificant to carry real weight. If you rely solely on LinkedIn or a resume, you risk making decisions based on exaggerated or ambiguous signals rather than meaningful experience.

That's why the matching process demands a deep dive into every role a Fractional Executive has held in their career. At Vendux, we hold long-form onboarding conversations, often 90 minutes, to uncover the real details: What problems has this executive solved? What scenarios have they navigated? What were the complexities?

Executives frequently forget to mention important challenges they've overcome simply because they don't view those experiences as noteworthy. When we ask the right questions, those stories surface, and they're often crucial to achieving the right match.

2) Stage Appropriateness

When we talk about stage appropriateness for Fractional Executives, we're referring to the company's growth stage.

In the startup and scale-up world, particularly in tech and SaaS, each revenue band represents a distinct operating environment. What works at $0–1M is very different from what's required at $1–5M, $5–20M, or $20–100M. The priorities change, the levers shift, and the available resources vary dramatically.

A Fractional Executive must have experience operating within the same growth stage their client currently occupies. Otherwise, the learning curve becomes a distraction, and the executive risks recommending solutions that don't align with the organization's maturity level.

Ownership structure is another form of "stage" that matters. Family-owned and family-run businesses operate very differently from private-equity-backed companies, venture-backed startups, or publicly traded corporations. Each structure comes with its own decision-making patterns, pressures, time horizons, and quirks.

A Fractional Executive should have firsthand experience navigating whichever ownership model the client operates within. Without prior exposure, the executive loses effectiveness, becoming distracted by operating dynamics rather than focusing on functional work.

3) Cultural Compatibility

Culture fit is real, but culture must be interpreted correctly in the context of fractional work.

Because Fractional Executives are not full-time, permanent, or on-site, cultural compatibility should not overshadow functional fit. In fact, an overemphasis on likability, often the true meaning behind culture fit, can distract from what truly matters: whether the executive has solved this specific problem before.

Cultural fitness is not irrelevant, but it should come after functional qualifications. If a CEO senses something is "off," they should trust that instinct. Conversely, when multiple executives check every box, cultural alignment becomes a valid tiebreaker, especially because Fractionals work closely with CEOs and founders.

But Fractional Executives are not being hired to assimilate into a team's personality. Often, they are being hired because the team itself requires change.

"Culture fit" is real, but it should never be the primary filter for Fractional placements. Functional fit comes first. Stage and ownership context come next. Culture fit is a final "go/no-go" decision.

The CEO Problem:
"Someone from Our Industry" and "A Rock Star"

On the client side, CEOs frequently start their search with overly simplistic criteria. When asked what they're looking for, they often answer with two phrases:

1. "Someone from our industry," and
2. "A rock star."

Neither is meaningful.

To find the right leader, a founder, owner, or CEO must articulate the true nature of their problem. And that leads to the discovery of the specific skills required to solve it. Is the key factor industry familiarity? Product familiarity? Knowledge of the decision maker? Experience with a particular type of sale, such as transactional, enterprise, or strategic? What tools or systems need to be mastered? What level of complexity? What revenue model?

When a CEO can describe their sales motion, financial structure, or operational processes accurately and in detail, the likelihood of finding the right executive rises dramatically.

Fractional hiring is not about "potential." It's not about mentoring someone into the role or hoping they learn on the job. Fractional Executives are brought in because they have already done exactly what the CEO needs.

For example:

A fractional CFO must have built the exact kind of financial insights the company lacks.
A fractional CRO must have navigated the exact type of sales motion the company runs.

A fractional CMO must have executed the exact type of go-to-market strategy the company requires.

It's about specificity, not generality.

The Matching Process: Recruiting Done Right

Fractional Executives are an invaluable resource for companies facing skills gaps, launching new initiatives, conserving limited resources, and addressing critical priorities. These professionals offer an effective alternative to traditional recruiting, consulting, or training, and certainly surpass the option of doing nothing and hoping for the best.

The key to their success lies in finding the perfect match, in other words, bringing in someone who has "been there and done that."

Here is how that matching process should work when it's done correctly:

Step 1: Defining Job Specifications ("Criteria")

The roles and responsibilities for a Fractional Executive differ from those in a traditional executive recruiting process for a permanent hire. The need for such leadership typically arises from unique situations that require immediate, focused action and a significant re-prioritization of regular business responsibilities.

When defining job specifications, the focus should be on the immediate needs and the work to be accomplished in the next three, six, or nine months. This might involve overseeing the normal course of business but often requires something extra or different.

Therefore, it is crucial not to recycle old job descriptions used for permanent searches. Instead, be prepared for unexpected topics and questions that will help identify the Fractional Executive's main priorities.

The criteria should also focus on the specific, relevant past experiences that will make the executive successful. For a Fractional Sales Leader, for example, this includes describing the sales scenario in greater detail, including target personas, deal structure, and length of sales cycle.

Step 2: The Search ("Matching")

Finding the perfect Fractional Executive is not a sped-up version of traditional executive recruiting.

There is a pool of mid-career, experienced executives eager to take on hands-on projects at great companies. These executives are vetted and ready to be matched with the right opportunities.

The matching process involves aligning job specifications with the roster of available executives, resulting in a tight slate of one or two highly qualified candidates. There is no need to cast a wide net or process a large funnel of candidates. That saves time and resources and increases match quality.

Step 3: The Final Selection ("Interview")

Clarifying and streamlining the selection process before beginning the interviews is crucial. The goal is to move quickly, make smart decisions, and secure buy-in from the right stakeholders.

Identify the primary decision-maker and manage the expectations of other stakeholders. Not everyone in the organization needs to be involved in the decision or meet the executive before their selection, but the process should be decisive and focused on filling the recognized void.

Step 4: Compensation ("Investment")

When considering compensation, think about the overall value to your business of filling the skills gap.

Fractional Executives often command higher cash compensation than permanent hires due to the urgency and complexity of the situations they address. However, it's important to accurately compare the overall costs and benefits.

With a Fractional Executive, a business does not incur any of the indirect costs associated with permanent employees, such as benefits, holidays, sick days, bonuses, equity, training, and equipment.

Fractional Executives also offer the flexibility to pay only for the services needed, whether that's a few hours a week or more.

Timing, Decision Cycles, and External Uncertainty

With clear communication on both sides, the matching process becomes more effective and faster. At Vendux, the average time from intake to placement is about 20 days. Our matching algorithm identifies candidates instantly, but we still speak with each executive to confirm interest and availability.

The longest part of the cycle, though, is the client's internal interview process. Even with perfect matches, clients typically want to compare at least two candidates, involve multiple stakeholders, and conduct a second or third round of conversations. Most of the timeline is client-driven rather than match-driven.

When clients delay decisions, it's often due to external uncertainty. We've seen companies reach the finish line only to hesitate due to economic uncertainty.

End-of-year timing also varies by industry. Construction companies often slow down over the winter months. Other sectors, such as fitness, have peak seasons beginning January 1st and must have systems and leadership in place before the year turns.

Understanding these timelines helps align the matching process with the company's operational calendar.

Character and Behavior: The Data People Don't Put on LinkedIn

Executives highlight achievements, not failures or misalignments. No one writes, "I was fired," or "The job was nothing like what was promised," or "I had a mediocre performance record in this job." But those experiences matter. They reveal how someone handles conflict, adapts to bad environments, or navigates misrepresentation, skills that often define how they'll operate in a challenging fractional engagement.

This is also why we observe their behavior during our interactions:

- Do they show up on time?
- Do they cancel repeatedly?
- Do they dominate conversations without asking questions?
- Are they overly self-focused, or do they demonstrate reflective thinking?

These patterns matter because they reflect how the executive will engage with a CEO and a team.

As part of our own process, we introduced a character assessment, measuring six traits:

- Integrity
- Humility
- Accountability
- Respect
- Confidence
- Grit

The assessment includes a self-evaluation, evaluations from references provided by the Executive, and independent evaluations from connections we identify ourselves.

We don't use the assessment to eliminate candidates; rather, we use it as an additional data point to strengthen match accuracy and proactively address CEO concerns. The alignment or misalignment between these perspectives reveals self-awareness, reliability, work ethic, and consistency of behavior.

But again: none of these traits is one-size-fits-all. A talkative personality may be a perfect fit for one client and a terrible fit for another. A reserved, highly analytical style may be ideal in some contexts but ineffective in others.

The key is alignment with the specific situation and the specific leader.

The "No Learning Curve" Principle—and Why It's Harder Now

Another key principle for the process is that there is (almost) no learning curve build into a fractional engagement. Founders, owners, and CEOs are not paying for someone to learn their craft. A Fractional Executive must be effective almost immediately.

Yes, they must learn about the company, its people, and its product, but that's orientation, not skill acquisition. An experienced Fractional Executive has gone through multiple "orientations" in their career. And the ability to step in quickly is directly tied to whether the executive has confronted this exact scenario before.

Fractional Executives must stay current, especially as AI tools are transforming every business function. In earlier decades, mastering the CRM or the ERP was enough. Today, a leader must understand a tech stack of 10 to 15 interconnected tools, many of them AI-driven. Staying current is no longer optional; it is a core requirement.

Fractional Executives must continuously educate themselves, take demos, experiment with tools, and study new technologies to avoid falling years behind. In a full-time role, companies provide the training and exposure. In fractional work, this responsibility falls entirely onto the Executive. Without active learning, even the best past experience quickly loses relevance.

The Relevant Market for a Matchmaker

Staffing Industry Analysts (SIA) published a report on the talent platform landscape. How does a company like Vendux fit into the space?

Globally, B2B talent platforms in 2023 reached $16.0B in gross spend volume (fees paid to workers plus fees for facilitating transactions)[23]. Gross spending volume in the U.S. alone totaled $6.2B.

SIA differentiates three platform categories, all part of the gig economy:

- **Work services platforms** are responsible for the outcome rather than the labor relationship. Examples include Uber and DoorDash.
- **Temporary staffing platforms** incorporate traditional staffing services such as performing background checks, onboarding, and time tracking. Examples are Allegis and Randstad.
- **Talent platforms** connect clients with freelancers not employed by the platform. Examples are Upwork[24] and Fiverr.

---

[23] https://www.staffingindustry.com/news/global-daily-news/talent-platform-market-gross-spend-falls-for-first-time

[24] https://www.upwork.com/

So, where does Vendux fit?

Competition law is known to define a "relevant market." It comprises all those products and/or services that are regarded as interchangeable or substitutable by the client by reason, among others, of the products' characteristics and their intended use.

In light of this definition, here are a few thoughts:

- Vendux is not a work services platform. We connect people, not outcomes. Even though many executive engagements are entered with a specific outcome in mind.
- Vendux is not a temporary staffing platform, even though our contracting, billing, and executive payment model is very similar.
- Vendux is not a talent platform, at least not in the sense of an online self-service model. We take pride in our white-glove service.

Some of our service characteristics and intended use are similar to temporary staffing and talent platforms:

- Our contracting, billing, and executive payment model is similar to temporary staffing.
- We facilitate the entire process on behalf of clients, from sourcing to billing.
- We match freelancing talent that addresses a skill or resource gap at the client.

So, if and where we fit might be in the eye of the beholder.

Knowing that clients can use a variety of solutions to address their sales and growth challenges, the relevant market is certainly larger and includes those platforms, as well as other solution providers.

The PerfectMatch™

There is a common saying: "There's a lid for every pot."

Its original meaning is romantic: somewhere in the world, there is a compatible partner for everybody.

In the world of business, though, finding the perfect fit between an Executive and a company can often feel like searching for a needle in a haystack. The stakes are high; misaligned leadership can stifle growth, disrupt team harmony, and even lead to financial setbacks.

This is where the concept of Fractional Leadership comes into play, providing companies with a flexible, effective solution that matches leadership to specific business needs. But even within this model, the challenge remains: How do you find the match that is not merely "good," but actually right?

Enter our proprietary PerfectMatch™ system, which matches businesses with the ideal Fractional Leader.

Fractional Leadership has emerged as a powerful trend, particularly among small- to medium-sized companies and startups. The concept is simple: instead of hiring a full-time executive, companies bring on an experienced leader on a part-time basis.

This allows organizations to access top-tier talent without the commitment or cost of a full-time hire. Fractional Leaders bring their expertise to specific areas such as sales, marketing, finance, and operations, helping companies navigate challenges, drive growth, and achieve strategic goals.

However, the success of this model hinges on one critical factor: **finding the right leader.**

A leader with stellar credentials on paper may not always be the right fit for the company's culture, market, or specific needs. The challenge is not just to find a Fractional Leader, but to find the Fractional Leader who is perfectly aligned with the company's unique requirements.

The PerfectMatch™ system operates on a few core principles:

1. **Comprehensive understanding of business needs**: an in-depth assessment of the company's current situation, challenges, goals, culture, and long-term vision.

2. **Leader profiling**: experience, skill sets, track record, leadership style, adaptability, character, and prior exposure to very similar business scenarios.

3. **Flexibility and scalability**: the system accommodates evolving needs—early-stage growth, stabilization, market entry, or transformation.

In a crowded marketplace, PerfectMatch™ stands out for its rigor. It's not just about finding a leader who can do the job; it's about finding the leader who will excel in that role, within that specific company, at that particular time, and with those specific challenges.

Perfect matches are built, not found.

How Depth and Breadth Fuel the Match

At Vendux, we've surpassed a milestone that not only reflects our growth but also significantly enhances the value we bring to every client engagement. Our roster in early 2026 includes more than 1,400 pre-vetted, senior-level sales executives.

The number itself is not the point. What it enables matters: great precision, faster matches, and better outcomes for businesses looking to build, fix, or scale their sales operations.

More than a number; it's a strategic advantage.

Crossing the 1,000 mark in 2025 was not symbolic. It's the result of years of rigorous vetting, market insight, and relationship-building. Our bench covers executives in sales, revenue, commercial, business development, and growth; in the field, inside, eCommerce, operations, enablement, and partnership. Each comes with a proven track record and readiness to step into fractional, interim, advisory, or consulting roles.

When a company partners with Vendux, they're not just accessing talent. They're tapping into a curated marketplace of sales leadership.

A deep talent pool is only valuable if it's searchable and scannable with purpose. That's where PerfectMatch™ becomes operational: it goes beyond superficial keywords or job titles and considers business challenges, sales scenarios, strategic goals, team dynamics, and growth stage, then matches them with executives whose experience aligns with each dimension.

It's not about "good enough." It's about "exactly right."

And timing matters as much as talent. When a business loses a sales leader unexpectedly, faces stalled growth, or enters a critical go-to-market window, waiting months to recruit simply isn't viable. A pre-vetted network allows urgent response without sacrificing quality.

Questions Each Side Should Ask the Other

The final layer of matchmaking is not sourcing or screening. It is the diagnostic part of the interview.

Questions to Ask: Executive → Client

Fractional Executives must ask a comprehensive list of diagnostic questions. These are similar to the questions we ask during our executive intake calls at Vendux.

Executives cannot rely on founders, owners, and CEOs to volunteer critical context; many CEOs are hiring a Fractional for the first time and don't yet know what matters. The executive must lead the discovery process to understand scope, expectations, metrics, challenges, decision-making dynamics, and history.

Questions to Ask: Client → Executive

For founders, owners, and CEOs, the Fractional Leadership Alliance has published guidance, including *Red Flags When Hiring Fractional Executives*[25], with suggested interview questions tied to specific warning signs.

CEOs should use the interview process with Fractional Executives to quickly assess whether the candidate can deliver senior-level impact in compressed timeframes, not merely provide extra hands. The guide highlights four areas that strong interview questions should probe:

- Depth of experience
- Strategic thinking
- Working style
- Realistic capacity

Effective Fractionals have already held comparable full-time leadership roles, built and led teams, and operated at or beyond the company's current growth stage. They demonstrate curiosity by asking thoughtful questions, can discuss failures and learning, and clearly articulate the tools and processes they use to get traction quickly.

---

[25] https://www.fractionalleadershipalliance.com/thought-leadership

From a fit perspective, CEOs should look for executives who focus on outcomes, are willing to share insights, and are comfortable in constructively challenging leadership. Finally, capacity and conflicts of interest must be addressed directly to ensure the executive can commit sufficient time, especially in the early months. Ultimately, the interview should confirm both competence and mutual fit, as successful fractional engagements require rapid trust, alignment, and execution.

For example, if an executive has spent 20–30 years in one narrow industry vertical, they may struggle to apply their skills in a new environment. The recommended question is:

"Tell me about a time you transferred a skill from one industry to another."

If their answer stays within one vertical, for example the transfer of a skill from one SaaS company to another, you quickly learn whether they can actually adapt.

Because founders, owners, and CEOs are inexperienced at assessing fractional talent, the burden of clarity falls more heavily on the executive. Still, CEOs need guidance on identifying true competence. That is why the Fractional Leadership Alliance focuses so much on equipping founders, owners, and CEOs with the right tools.

Fit Is Built, Not Found

Ultimately, matching executives with companies requires depth, specificity, rigor, and a role-by-role understanding of what success actually looks like.

A LinkedIn profile cannot reveal that.
A resume cannot reveal that.

Only a detailed, structured, scenario-based evaluation, combined with a clear understanding of the founder, owner, or CEO's problem, the executive's genuine experience, and the realities of the company's timing and environment, can provide a reliable basis for decision-making.

Case Example:
Same Executive, Two Outcomes

One of the most instructive lessons in fractional work is this: even with the same executive, the same matching process, and the same best practices in place, two engagements can unfold in completely different ways.

At the time of this writing, one Fractional Executive was working simultaneously in two assignments sourced through the same platform, using the same vetting criteria, role scoping, and matching methodology. On paper, both engagements looked sound. In reality, they could not have diverged more sharply.

In one company, the engagement was thriving. The executive was operating squarely within her strengths. A clear strategy had been agreed upon. The CEO trusted her judgment, gave her space to lead, and aligned expectations with the realities of the market. As a result, the pipeline was strong, deals were moving toward close, and momentum was clearly building. The signals of success—traction, confidence, and shared clarity—were all there.

In the other company, the engagement struggled almost immediately.

The issue was not effort, capability, or commitment on the executive's part. Instead, it was a growing misalignment between what the CEO wanted and what the executive had actually been hired to do. Over time, the messages coming from the client and the messages coming from the executive began to diverge. Each side believed they were being reasonable. Each side believed the other was missing something.

On its face, this might sound like a tactical disagreement. In reality, it revealed a deeper problem. The executive had not been hired—or priced—to function in low level execution. She had been brought in for strategic revenue leadership. Asking her to perform high-volume outbound activity was not only outside the original scope, but it was also a misuse of both her expertise and the company's budget.

Even more critically, the company was selling high-value consulting services—six-figure engagements. Cold calling is rarely an effective primary channel for selling complex, trust-based, high-ticket offerings. The issue wasn't just role misfit; it was a go-to-market strategy that was unlikely to succeed regardless of who executed it.

At that point, the only responsible path forward was a brutally honest conversation:

This work was outside the agreed scope, misaligned with her strengths, and unlikely to deliver the results the CEO was hoping for. From there, the decision belonged to the CEO. Either return to the original strategy—one aligned with the executive's skills and the nature of the business—or acknowledge that the desired approach required a different type of resource altogether.

In other words, there were only two viable paths forward. Continue with a model designed for success, or part ways and pursue a fundamentally different approach with someone better suited to that work.

What makes this case so important is not that one engagement struggled. That happens. What matters is the contrast. The same executive, operating at the same time, was producing excellent results in one environment and facing resistance in another. The difference was not talent. It was alignment.

This case underscores a critical truth of Fractional Leadership: matching well is necessary, but it is not sufficient. Even the best executive will fail if expectations drift, scope is ignored, or the CEO is unwilling to adjust assumptions. Fractional work succeeds not because everything goes according to plan, but because when things go off plan, leaders are willing to confront reality quickly, honestly, and decisively.

That willingness—not the resume, not the process—is often what determines whether an engagement recovers or ends.

CHAPTER 12

Shared Accountability: How Engagements Succeed

Fractional Leadership works best when it is understood for what it is: a shared responsibility. While some aspects of a fractional engagement clearly belong to one side or the other, as outlined throughout this book, the outcomes themselves are never owned by the executive or the founder, owner, or CEO alone. They are built together.

This chapter focuses on that joint responsibility and how fractional engagements are scoped, governed, adjusted, monitored, and ultimately concluded in a way that creates lasting enterprise value rather than short-term relief.

Setting the Foundation: Scoping the Engagement Together

Every successful fractional engagement begins with clear scoping. This is not a formality; it is the foundation on which everything else rests.

Here, some responsibilities are naturally distinct. Fractional Executives must ask the right diagnostic questions, pressure-test assumptions, and help define what success should look like. CEOs, founders, and owners must provide accurate context, including honest assessments of constraints, priorities, internal dynamics, and financial realities.

But scoping itself is a shared exercise.

Clarity is required around:

- The core problems to be solved

- The desired outcomes
- The expected timeline
- The level of executive involvement required

Fractional roles are not generic. They are situational. A company may need transformation, stabilization, or simply momentum. Without shared clarity on which problem is being addressed, even a highly capable executive can start to drift.

This is also where flexibility must be built in from the start. Markets shift. Priorities change. What looks like the right problem to address in month one may not be the most urgent issue in month three. A well-scoped engagement anticipates that reality rather than resisting it.

Contracts, Governance, and Shared Accountability

Once the scope is defined, structure matters.

Contracts in fractional engagements are not just legal instruments; they are alignment tools. Retainers, milestones, termination clauses, and flexibility provisions should reflect the reality that fractional work evolves over time.

Several elements in this process are inherently joint responsibilities:

- Contracting requires agreement from both sides.
- KPI definition and reporting require shared commitment.
- Governance and communication cadence must be co-created.
- Pivots—whether incremental or material—must be mutually decided.

Governance is particularly critical. Clear reporting lines, defined KPIs, and scheduled review cycles prevent confusion and reduce conflict. In healthy engagements, these mechanisms are not used to control or micromanage, but to ensure transparency and momentum.

And when communication is consistent and review cycles are honored, course corrections rarely feel dramatic. Both sides tend to recognize the need for pivots simultaneously.

Delivering Outcomes Together: Ownership Without Micromanagement

Fractional engagements often fail at the extremes, either through micromanagement or absenteeism.

When founders, owners, or CEOs over-manage, Fractional Executives are reduced to expensive operators rather than strategic leaders. When founders, owners, and CEOs disengage entirely, executives lack the authority and context needed to drive change.

The balance lies in the joint ownership of outcomes.

Fractional Executives are responsible for execution within their mandate. Founders, owners, and CEOs remain responsible for prioritization, decision-making, and organizational support. Neither role works in isolation.

Mid-engagement reviews play a critical role here. These are not performance reviews in the traditional sense; they are alignment checkpoints. What's working? What's not? What assumptions have changed? What needs to be adjusted?

Handled well, these reviews strengthen trust and accelerate results rather than introducing tension.

Engagement Monitoring and Early Intervention

Vendux stays lightly connected throughout active engagements. Early on, monthly check-ins are often appropriate. As engagements stabilize, that cadence may shift to larger intervals.

When issues arise, they unfortunately tend to fall into predictable categories:

- Communication breakdowns
- Mismatched expectations
- Personality or working-style friction

The purpose of monitoring is not oversight; it is early detection. Small misalignments are far easier to address than entrenched frustration.

Functionality issues are far less common. Financial failure, when a client simply runs out of capital, is one of the few problems that cannot be solved through better alignment. In rare cases, rates or hours may be adjusted to preserve continuity, but most financial breakdowns ultimately end the engagement.

Planning the Exit:
Designing the End at the Beginning

One of the most overlooked aspects of fractional work is exit planning. Every fractional engagement should assume an eventual transition, even if the timeline is uncertain.

Exits generally fall into three categories:

1. **Transition to a full-time executive**
   Fractional Leaders are often uniquely positioned to help identify and onboard their full-time successor. They understand the role in practice, not just theory.
2. **Handoff to an internal team member**
   In some cases, an internal leader has been developed and is ready to step into the role.

3. **Completion of a project-based engagement**
    Some fractional assignments are designed to end once a
    deliverable—such as a comprehensive sales playbook—is
    completed and implemented.

Regardless of the scenario, knowledge transfer is essential. Documentation captures part of it, but not all. Institutional knowledge, judgment calls, and historical context must be intentionally handed off to avoid regression.

We recommend that both sides insist on a closing conversation. This is not a formal exit interview, but a structured debrief designed to capture:

- What went well
- What didn't
- What could have been done differently
- Key accomplishments
- Outstanding risks or unfinished areas

Fractional Executives should also use this phase to request testimonials and referrals, reinforcing continuity beyond the engagement.

From Solving Problems to Creating Enterprise Value

Solving an immediate problem is not the same as creating durable value.

A sales playbook, for example, is a deliverable, but it does not generate revenue on its own. Value comes from implementation, coaching, and reinforcement. In many cases, the highest return comes from extending the relationship into a lighter support model, such as a few hours per week of coaching a newly hired salesperson or quarterly reviews of pipeline health.

The same pattern appears in finance, marketing, and operations. A fractional CFO may build the right financial system and train the leadership team. The primary project ends, but periodic reviews ensure insights continue to drive decisions.

Fractional work often concludes in two phases:

- **Transition**, overlapping with a full-time hire or internal successor
- **Sustainability support**, through coaching, check-ins, or advisory involvement

This continuity is where fractional engagements evolve from tactical fixes into strategic investments.

Knowing When to Transition

Fractional Leadership is a growth accelerator, but it is rarely meant to be permanent. Exceptions include companies in very small niches that will never grow to a size that requires a full-time-equivalent executive.

Fractional Executives are most effective when:

- Leadership is needed quickly
- The business is not yet ready for full-time cost or commitment
- Systems, structure, or direction must be built in the early phases of scaling

Over time, however, signals emerge that the business has outgrown the fractional model:

- Growth requires constant executive oversight
- Investors or boards push for full-time leadership
- Teams become dependent on executives with limited availability
- The function becomes central to ongoing value creation

Recognizing this inflection point is critical. Done poorly, transitions stall progress. Done well, they feel like graduation.

Planning the Shift to Full-Time Leadership

The transition from fractional to full-time should be intentional, not abrupt.

Best practices include:

- Engaging the Fractional Executive in defining the full-time role
- Codifying playbooks, KPIs, processes, and frameworks before transition
- Gathering feedback from internal teams
- Considering a step-down advisory model for the Fractional during the handoff

Fractional Executives who help design their own succession leave behind stronger organizations and often remain trusted partners long after their primary role ends.

Shared Responsibility, Shared Success

Fractional Leadership is not a shortcut. It is a disciplined, collaborative approach to building capability at the right moment in a company's evolution.

When both parties understand their joint responsibilities, including scoping clearly, governing thoughtfully, reviewing honestly, and exiting intentionally, the result is not just progress, but momentum that carries forward.

Handled well, fractional engagements don't just fill gaps. They prepare businesses for their next chapter.

PART IV

The Future of Fractional Leadership

CHAPTER 13

The Blended Workforce and Beyond

When considering the future of Fractional Leadership, it's important to recognize that Fractional Executives are part of a broader category of organizational innovation. Scholars often refer to this as a subset of "organizational innovation trends," which include remote work, hybrid structures, gig talent, and flexible work arrangements. The workplace today is in the midst of one of the greatest transformations since the Industrial Revolution. Traditional employment models, full-time roles, long-term careers at a single company, and offices filled with permanent staff are giving way to something far more flexible and dynamic. This shift is not simply about remote work or digital collaboration; it is about the emergence of a blended workforce.

A blended workforce combines full-time employees with a mix of gig workers, freelancers, Fractional Leaders, and artificial intelligence. It is a model defined less by rigid job titles and more by outcomes, agility, and access to the right expertise at the right time. Several forces have converged to accelerate this move toward a blended workforce:

- Gig economy and freelancing: Millions of professionals now operate independently, selling specialized expertise on demand.
- Remote and hybrid models: Work-from-anywhere has become normalized, unlocking global talent pools.
- Unbundling or fractionalizing of roles: Instead of one person holding a monolithic position, companies increasingly split responsibilities across multiple experts.
- Technological acceleration: AI tools are reshaping tasks, automating processes, and collaborating with humans to amplify productivity.

- Fractional Leadership: Senior executives are no longer tied exclusively to one organization. They bring leadership as a service, guiding multiple companies on a part-time, interim, or project basis.

Together, these forces are dissolving the traditional walls of the workplace. Companies that once relied solely on employees now have access to an ecosystem of contributors, each adding value in different ways and at different times.

Within this broader shift toward a blended workforce, not all roles carry the same strategic weight, and it is here that Fractional Executives distinguish themselves.

Fractional Executives at the Top of the Pyramid

Fractional Executives sit at the top of this innovation pyramid not because they're more important than other roles, but because they occupy the uppermost positions on organizational charts. A blended workforce is not simply outsourcing or hiring contractors. It is a deliberate design where different talent types coexist and complement one another. Imagine a company where:

Full-time employees provide stability and continuity.

- Freelancers deliver creative, technical, or project-based skills on demand.
- Fractional Executives guide strategy, growth, and transformation without the overhead of full-time C-suite hires.
- AI agents handle repetitive or analytical tasks, freeing humans to focus on higher-value work.

The result is a talent mosaic, fluid, adaptive, and capable of scaling up or down with market demands. And doing so with far less disruption than the traditional approach of large-scale, full-time hiring and firing.

Within this model, Fractional Executives occupy a particularly strategic position. Unlike freelancers who execute narrowly defined tasks, Fractional Executives bring leadership, vision, and accountability to key business functions, including sales, marketing, operations, and finance. They are the connective tissue in a blended workforce. A fractional CRO, for example, can lead a team of full-time reps, coordinate marketing freelancers, and deploy AI-enabled analytics to refine go-to-market strategies, all while working fractionally across multiple organizations. This flexibility provides companies with immediate access to top-tier leadership without the financial commitment of a full-time executive. It also allows businesses to adapt leadership capacity to growth stages, investor expectations, or market shifts.

The gig economy overall is massive, with millions of workers operating as freelancers, contractors, and project-based specialists. In contrast, Fractional Executives are a small but fast-growing segment, perhaps 200,000 to 300,000 globally in 2025, with roughly 80,000 in North America, where the trend began. That number continues to rise as fractional work moves beyond its original home in tech and SaaS into more traditional industries.

Market Size, Demand, and Adoption Rates

Estimating the size of the fractional marketplace is difficult. You could approach it by examining income: if 80,000 executives in North America earn an average of $200,000 annually, the supply-side market size becomes visible. But that doesn't necessarily reflect the true market, because opportunity far exceeds current utilization.

Historically, the industry has often cited the claim that "25% of companies have used a Fractional Executive," but that figure lacks a verifiable source. In my experience I estimate that a more realistic scenario is closer to 15% overall adoption across U.S. companies in 2025. However, there's a sharp divide:

- Tech & SaaS: 70–80% adoption
- General SMB economy: 5–10% adoption

Fractional Leadership originated in tech and has steadily expanded into other industries. As more founders, owners, and CEOs become aware of the model and Fractional roles normalize, the market will naturally expand. Based on observed trends, we predict that fractional adoption will eventually reach approximately 40% of small- to medium-sized B2B businesses, reshaping how SMBs engage with senior leadership.

Risks and Potential Downward Trends

The greatest risk to the fractional industry is mislabeling; people calling themselves Fractional Executives without ever having held true senior leadership roles. Fractional Executives must genuinely qualify as executives, meaning they have led a functional area at the highest level, regardless of their title. When individuals without that background market themselves as Fractionals, they undermine the model's reputation. A founder, owner, or CEO who hires an underqualified person may conclude that Fractional Leadership "doesn't work," which harms everyone in the ecosystem.

Other risks include shifts toward AI or the return-to-office trend. But these pressures affect full-time executives at least as much, if not more. Fractional Leaders tend to operate remotely, but if a company requires on-site presence, the search simply narrows geographically. It is not a threat to the long-term viability of Fractional Leadership.

Economic downturns neither automatically translate into increased fractional demand nor into a decrease. While some argue that companies may "fractionalize" during tight times, in reality:

- If a role cannot be fractionalized, companies simply don't hire.
- Corporate layoffs do not create Fractional openings; they merely reduce roles overall.

Fractional roles thrive where fractionalization is structurally logical, not merely where budgets are tight.

Continuing Growth: Education, Awareness, and a Unified Voice

The continued adoption of Fractional Leadership depends heavily on education—helping founders, owners, and CEOs understand what Fractionals do, when the model works, and how to set up engagements for success. Vendux and Shiny, along with many other industry leaders and the Fractional Leadership Alliance, contribute to this effort through content, tools, and thought leadership. The industry's momentum over the last few years has been driven by that collective work, not by any single organization.

Yet the Fractional Executive sector remains fragmented, which is why a unified voice matters. The Fractional Leadership Alliance was created to bring organizations and Fractional Leaders together globally, elevate the model's value proposition and recognition, and advocate for shared interests.

At its best, an industry association serves as the connective infrastructure of a growing category: a platform for collaboration, knowledge sharing, and professional development; a vehicle for advocacy on standards and policies; and a steward for ethics, best practices, and accountability. Just as importantly, it helps translate the model for the broader business community by spotlighting outcomes, real success stories, and case studies that make the value of Fractional Leadership tangible, credible, and easier to adopt.

Specialization:
A Major Opportunity in the Blended Model

One of the most powerful trends is the move toward increased specialization. Traditional full-time roles often bundle several unrelated responsibilities together because founders, owners, and CEOs must justify the full-time salary. Hiring Fractionals allows companies to:

- Separate those responsibilities ("Fractionalize")
- Assign each to the right specialist
- Avoid compromises in skill sets

Here is a particularly relevant example in sales organizations. Companies frequently rely on "player-coach" roles: hybrid salespeople-managers who are part sales representative, part leader. These roles are rarely successful because they require two fundamentally different skill sets. Fractional specialization allows companies to hire:

- True sales leaders for strategy and coaching
- Individual contributors for selling

Industry-Level Threats, Innovation Cycles,
and One Real Barrier

Every innovation threatens someone. Gasoline engines threatened horse breeding; they are now threatened by electric vehicles, and those will soon be threatened by hydrogen. Platforms like Upwork and Fiverr threaten temp agencies. Fractional Leadership is simply part of this ongoing innovation cycle. Organizations that fail to adapt will be left behind. Those that evolve will thrive. The fractional model will not reverse or disappear; the trend is too entrenched and too aligned with modern workforce dynamics.

One legitimate challenge facing Fractional solopreneurs in the U.S. is health insurance. Employer-sponsored group coverage is subsidized, making it more affordable for full-time employees. Solopreneurs must purchase individual plans that are often expensive. A few organizations now offer group plans for solopreneurs, but they are early-stage and not quite large enough to offer substantial savings that match an employer's group coverage. As these groups grow, though, the cost will likely decrease.

This issue is unique to the U.S.; countries with universal healthcare don't face the same barrier. Still, this challenge is not existential. If health costs rise, health insurance rates for both full-time employees and Fractional Executives will rise accordingly. Over time, the market will rebalance and recognize the importance of the blended workforce.

While innovation cycles create disruption and opportunity, only a few challenges materially affect the Fractional model, and most are structural rather than existential.

Where This Goes Next

If the blended workforce is the operating model, Fractional Executives are the leadership layer that makes it coherent, especially as companies learn to orchestrate full-time teams, freelancers, and AI-enabled execution as one system. The future of work is not on the horizon; it has already arrived. The blended workforce is rapidly becoming the default operating model, especially for small- and medium-sized businesses.

Full-time employees will remain essential, but they will increasingly be surrounded by an ecosystem of Fractional Executives, gig workers, and intelligent AI systems.

More adoption in mid-market and enterprise. As more founders, owners, and CEOs become aware of the model and its advantages, and as Fractional roles become normalized, the market will naturally expand.

Growth of global fractional talent. As globalization and digital transformation continue, the demand for flexible executive talent is likely to grow, leading to broader adoption of the Fractional Executive model worldwide.

Increased fractionalization by industry or stage. Specialization allows companies to separate responsibilities, assign each to perfectly matched talent, and avoid compromises in skill sets, especially when growth stage, complexity, and operating context require precision rather than generality

Throughout this book, I have deliberately avoided silver bullets and shortcuts. Fractional Leadership works not because it is cheaper, trendier, or more flexible, but because it is intentional. The tactics discussed in *Right-Sized, Right-Skilled*™—clear positioning, disciplined scoping, value-based pricing, structured onboarding, proactive communication, and rigorous expectation management—are not optional extras. They are the operating system of a successful fractional engagement.

For Fractional Executives, success comes from knowing exactly what problem to solve, for whom, and under what conditions. It requires building a business around oneself with the same care you once applied to running someone else's. The most effective Fractionals are selective, prepared, transparent about their limits, and relentless about clarity. They do not win by being everything to everyone, but by being precisely right for a specific moment.

For companies, success comes from readiness. Fractional Leaders do not replace accountability, ownership, or hard decisions. They amplify them. Organizations that succeed with fractional talent are clear about their goals, honest about their constraints, and committed to partnership rather than delegation. They treat the engagement as leadership, not consulting.

When both sides do this work upfront, fractional engagements become transformative. Not because they last forever, but because they deliver exactly what is needed, when it matters most. That is where Fractional Leadership proves its real value.

And the final question for founders, owners, and CEOs is no longer whether they will adapt to the blended workforce; it is how quickly they will embrace it.